IMAGES OF THE
OLD WEST

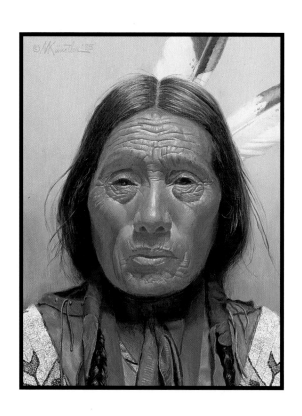

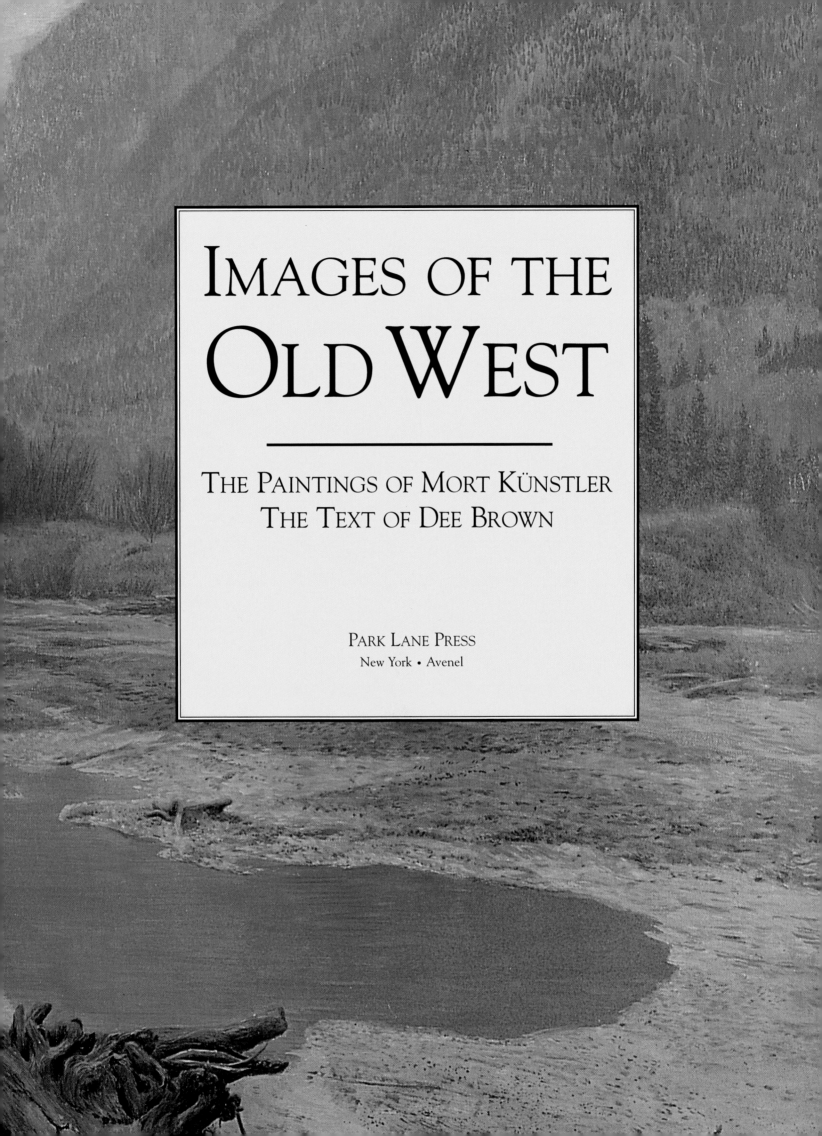

IMAGES OF THE
OLD WEST

THE PAINTINGS OF MORT KÜNSTLER
THE TEXT OF DEE BROWN

PARK LANE PRESS
New York • Avenel

For Deborah

A GLORYA HALE BOOK
This 1996 edition is published by Park Lane Press,
a division of Random House Value Publishing, Inc.,
40 Engelhard Avenue, Avenel, New Jersey 07001.

Park Lane Press and colophon are trademarks of
Random House Value Publishing, Inc.

Random House
New York • Toronto • London • Sydney • Auckland
http://www.randomhouse.com/

Designed by Liz Trovato

Printed and bound in the United States of America

Library of Congress Cataloging-in-Publication Data
Brown, Dee Alexander.
Images of the old West / the text of Dee Brown ;
the paintings of Mort Künstler.
p. cm.
ISBN 0-517-20012-0 (hardcover)
1. West (U.S.)—History. 2. Frontier and pioneer life—West (U.S.)
3. West (U.S.) in art. I. Künstler, Mort. II. Title.
F591.B875 1996
978—dc20   96-17079
                                                              CIP
10 9 8 7 6 5 4 3 2 1

With special thanks to:

Don Bender and Glorya Hale of Park Lane Press
for originating the idea for *Images of the Old West*. Their imagination
and vision have brought this book to fruition.

Dee Brown, the celebrated and highly esteemed author-historian,
for his wonderful text. Working with him has been a joy and I hope this
will lead to future collaborations.

Richard Lynch, director of Hammer Galleries in New York City,
who gave me my first one-man show in 1977. Nine more shows and a
lasting friendship have followed. My appreciation also to Howard Shaw and
the rest of the staff at Hammer Galleries.

Jane Künstler Broffman and Paula McEvoy, who have taken chaos
and turned it into order in a busy studio. I could not function without them.

And, of course, my dear Deborah,
my partner in every way.

CONTENTS

Daniel Boone

INTRODUCTION

The opening of the American West has created what the world now recognizes as this nation's greatest epic. Early on in the print media, and later in film and television, the popular images of the West have been fixed upon the area between the Mississippi River and the Pacific Ocean. The time period usually follows the Civil War to the end of the nineteenth century. Three centuries before this period of popular images, however, the American frontier had its beginning. During that earlier time, the new Americans were well aware of the boundless lands lying just over the horizon in the direction of the sun's setting.

The American West was here, of course, ten to twenty thousand years before any Europeans or Africans arrived. In the time charts of anthropologists, the American continents were very late in being occupied by human beings. Asians came first, by way of Alaska. Numerous and varied tribes were formed long before the Vikings or French fishermen, or Columbus and the Spaniards, saw the New World.

Less than twenty years after Columbus made his "discoveries," European adventurers were beginning to penetrate the coasts of the pristine land. In the vanguard were the Spaniards, exploring Florida and then coming north from Mexico into what is now the Southwestern United States. During this time Frenchmen explored the Mississippi Valley and founded New Orleans and St. Louis. When their fur trappers ventured into the Plains and the Rockies they were the first Europeans to learn the ways of the important Plains tribes. Some of their names still endure on the rolls of western tribes. Lewis and Clark met one of them: Charbonneau, the philandering husband of Sacagawea, the Shoshone woman who helped them find their way to the Pacific.

All through the eighteenth century, Russians were exploring the Pacific Coast from Alaska down to California, occasionally establishing trading posts; the Russian czars were not inclined to finance settlements, for Russia already had more land than people. Suspicious of Russian intentions, however, the Spaniards in Mexico sent Gaspar de Portola and Father Juniper Serra north to San Diego, Monterey, and San Francisco Bay to establish posts and missions.

Had Spain possessed a more abundant population, the American West likely would have become a Spanish-speaking land. But there simply were not enough Spaniards to settle all the vast territory the nation claimed, and their attempts to make colonists of native peoples failed from the start.

For the English-speaking people, the American West began at the Atlantic Coast. As land for farms and towns was taken from the inhabitants, the tide of the settlement moved west, slowly at first, and then at an accelerating pace. At every opportunity the British and their descendants took advantage of other European claimants, absorbing or seizing territories from them when for some reason or another they failed to hold fast.

By the beginning of the nineteenth century, the flow westward had become so variable, so uneven, that easterners were uncertain where the West began or even where it was. In 1830, when George Catlin, the artist, made his first journey westward, easterners thought that Buffalo and Niagara Falls were in the West. The inhabitants of Buffalo, however, believed the West began in Cincinnati, while the Cincinnati folk in turn perceived St. Louis as the West. At

St. Louis the West was somewhere up the broad Missouri. "It flies before us," said Catlin, "a phantom traveling on a timeless wing…. A country whose fascination spreads a charm over the mind almost dangerous to civilized pursuits."

The Old West, our mythological and mystical American past, still spreads a charm over the mind. Out of that experience has come the world's image of the romantic American—self-reliant, an overcomer of obstacles, generous but guarded, unsophisticated, friendly, righteous, expectant, impetuous, contradictory.

The frontier experience transformed many women who went there and endured. A determination to survive in harsh conditions brought with it the realization that they could sustain themselves, independent of others. They quickly cast off shackles of laws and customs that had confined them as chattel in the East or in Europe. They won the right to vote, to serve on juries, to own property, to earn their livings in pursuits once restricted to males.

From the time the world first became aware of the American West, people everywhere have been fascinated by its realities and illusions. Even in the early years, the first maps, early drawings of scenery, the native tribes, their costumes, reports of explorations, and guidebooks were in constant demand. And still the world never tires of covered wagons, cowboys, cattle drives, horse herds, trail towns, dance-hall girls; or the romance of transportation across the Plains and the Rockies—freight wagons, stagecoaches, pack horses, railroad building, early Pullman cars, steam locomotives; or by tales of lawmen and outlaws, bank robbers, gunfights and hangings, and the larger conflicts that brought bloody violence—the Indian wars, the range wars; or stories of the remarkable men and women, the peoples of many races who brought good and evil to the Western land.

Thousands of volumes have told variations of the Western story in words and pictures. Collections of photographs and illustrations have been brought together to depict the great legend. This book, however, is the first in which one artist portrays his vision of the Old West from its beginnings to its close. Mort Künstler's art is known for its graphic realism and vivid detail. He has spent a lifetime studying costumes and gear, the appurtenances of different periods of our past. And in almost every painting he tells a story, adding another dimension to the great American saga.

DEE BROWN

CHIEF HIGH HORSE

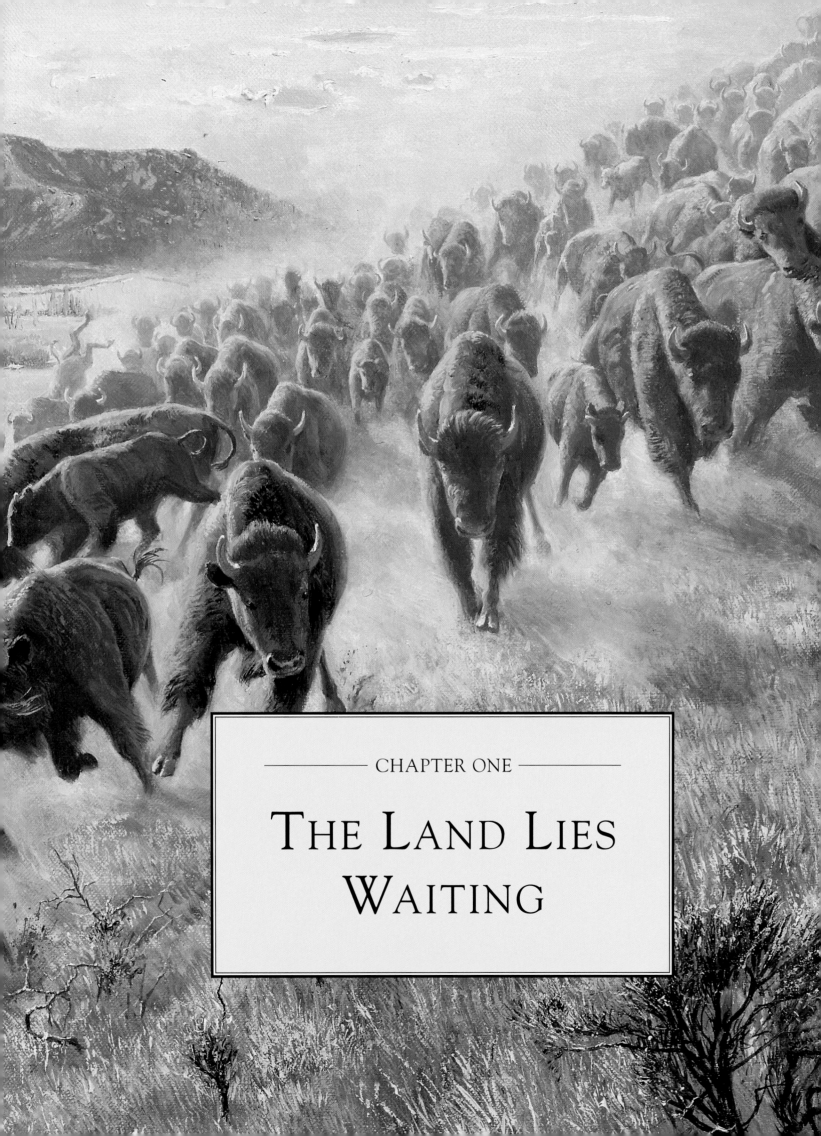

CHAPTER ONE

THE LAND LIES
WAITING

Before Europeans came to America, the native tribes lived on the coastlands or along streams. Among these tribes there was a great variation in language, physical appearance, dress, custom, diet, economy, religion, and attitudes. They formed a diverse continental population that had probably originated in Asia some thousands of years earlier.

In what is now the Southwestern United States, the Zunis and other Pueblo tribes lived in stone and adobe villages and managed to survive in an arid land. North of the Pueblos were the Paiutes, an ancient group of peoples whose early existence was not unlike that of the cave dwellers of the Stone Age. Living in a harsh environment, when Europeans first saw them they had progressed to wickiups, rude temporary shelters. The Chippewa, or Ojibway, were woodland people prospering in the forests and waters of the Great Lakes country. The Haida, inhabiting islands off the coast of British Columbia, were not an agricultural people. They were blessed with a plentiful food supply from the sea, leaving them with leisure time for arts and crafts. They were carvers and painters, the premier makers of totem poles. They built excellent canoes and houses and held frequent feasts known as potlatches.

On the Great Plains the tribes lived in tepees made from hides of buffalo, an animal held sacred because it also supplied much of their food. Before the coming of horses, the Plains tribes used dogs as beasts of burden. The Sun Dance, in which some performers placed skewers under their chest muscles, was an annual renewal ceremony. In what is now the Southeastern United States, the Creeks and Cherokees lived advanced woodland-agricultural lives, which they were later forced to transfer to "Indian Territory." The symbolic and complex renewal ceremony of the Creeks became known as the Green Corn Dance.

These were only a few of the dissimilar peoples among the hundreds of tribes that lived in North America at the time of Columbus. They were as diverse as the peoples of the city-states and principalities of old Europe.

As adventurers from beyond the oceans traveled closer to the mainland of America, they heard and spread rumors of these peoples. Soon after Columbus made his first landfall, dozens of Spanish explorers were venturing into Florida and making forays into the shores of the Gulf of Mexico. Treasure was what most of them sought, and they found some in Mexico. One of the more farsighted Spaniards, Gregario de Villalobos, brought along six heifers and a young bull, all possessed of long sharp-pointed horns. From them and other progenitors down the centuries would come the great Longhorn herds of Texas.

Young men like Francisco Coronado, who had served as a bold dragoon in his early years, came to Mexico with visions of gold. After he heard legends of the Seven Cities of Cibola that were filled with riches somewhere in the north, he organized a grand expedition into what is now the Southwest of the United States. To supply beef for the expedition he added a herd of long-horned cattle.

Cibola proved to be Zuni pueblos of stone, with no gold or precious jewels. The Zunis were terrified of the Spaniards because many of these intruders were wearing armor and riding horses—animals the Pueblo Indians had never seen. At first they believed the cavalrymen were monsters with men's heads and the bodies of four-legged animals.

The people of the Zuni Pueblos soon lost their fear of horses, however, and discovered that killing a Spaniard's horse was almost the same as disarming him. Some of Coronado's horses were lost or stolen before the expedition returned to Mexico. The Pueblos never valued horses highly except as goods to be traded to

Among those who came early into what is now the Great Basin of the western United States were numbers of small tribes, generally grouped as Paiutes. During the Stone Age they lived somewhat like the cave dwellers of Europe. By the time the first Europeans arrived, the continent was filled with a multitude of tribes, with diverse cultures that had developed from their varied environments.

Renewal ceremonies of some California tribes differed from those of the eastern and Plains peoples. Instead of celebrations involving the entire tribe, individuals performed dances and rituals. Above, a member of a secret society of the Pomo tribe is head dancer in the Kuksu ceremony.

The Haida, one of the more distinctive tribes of the Pacific Coast, were far advanced in painting, carving wood, and building. Left, visiting members of the Eagle clan are being welcomed by the Raven clan with a bear dance, part of the annual potlatch ceremonies that include exchanges of gifts.

their neighbors, especially the Apaches. Although the Apaches' way of life was not completely transformed by horses, as was the Plains tribes', they did become more mobile. Many Apaches wore spurs, disdained by most American Indians, and they established a reputation for their skill at taming wild mounts.

After maltreating the Zunis, the Spaniards went off in search of treasures elsewhere. They fell into the hands of a trickster, whom they named El Turco because his headdress resembled that of a Turkish soldier. He was probably a Pawnee far from home. "The Turk" told Coronado of a city of gold called Quiviera and then led him and his men for hundreds of miles across the southern Plains, visiting such places as Palo Duro Canyon, destined to become a symbolic site in the Indian wars and a place of cattle ranching in the nineteenth century.

Somewhere in what is now Kansas, the Spaniards saw at a distance the grass houses of the Wichita tribe glittering in the yellow sunlight and were sure the grass was spun gold. After another month of floundering in search of the mythical city of gold, Coronado ordered the Turk put to death, and the disillusioned Spaniards started the long journey back to Mexico.

Not until the next century did the British and other Europeans come to the New World to stay. Most came not for gold but to colonize, first in New England and Virginia, and then in a gradual move westward from the Atlantic Coast. By the beginning of the nineteenth century, the American colonists had formed a new nation, and the American West was anywhere beyond the Alleghenies.

Spaniards were the first Europeans to enter the American Southwest. In 1541, Francisco Coronado led an expedition from Mexico in search of the mythical Seven Cities of Cibola, supposedly filled with gold and other riches. Instead of gold, Coronado found the Zunis, who were terrified by the Spaniards' horses, animals never seen by them before. After marching through what is now New Mexico, Texas, Oklahoma, and Kansas, a bitterly disappointed Coronado returned to Mexico. But soon other Spaniards went back to the Southwest to colonize, convert, and exploit the native tribes.

In 1803, President Thomas Jefferson purchased the Territory of Louisiana from a strapped French government. In one stroke of a pen the size of the United States was doubled, half a billion acres for less than three cents an acre.

Jefferson wasted no time in planning an expedition to explore this vast and unknown land to the shores of the Pacific Ocean. No maps existed beyond rough charts of the Missouri River from St. Louis to the villages of the friendly Mandans, who lived near the mouth of the Knife River in what is now North Dakota. Rumors persisted of monsters, giant mammoths, and bands of cannibals in the Rocky Mountains. Less was known about the territory than the astronauts of 1969 knew about the requirements and objectives of their flight to the moon.

To lead the expedition, President Jefferson chose his secretary, Meriwether Lewis. Lewis then chose William Clark to bear equal rank and responsibility as a partner in discovery. The three Virginians had known each other since their youths and each believed sincerely in the importance of the mission.

To prepare for the first stage of the journey up the Missouri River, Lewis and Clark set up camp at Wood River near St. Louis. They selected fourteen soldiers from the U.S. Army, nine hardy young frontiersmen from Kentucky, two French boatmen, Clark's black servant York, and a civilian interpreter named Drouillard. To complete this variegated assembly, Lewis brought his Newfoundland dog, Scannon, whose perilous experiences were to match those of his owner. The day of their departure was May 14, 1804, and depart they did in two pirogues and a fifty-five-foot keelboat equipped with a square sail and twenty-two oars.

Because their homeland was in Mexico and the Spanish Southwest, where spirited mounts were first brought from Europe by the Spaniards, the Apaches acquired horses before the Plains tribes. They became adept at rounding up and taming the animals, and traded them to northern and eastern tribes.

While serving as Spain's governor of the Californias, in 1769 Gaspar de Portola set out from San Diego with orders to establish a mission at Monterey. Overshooting Monterey, he marched on to San Francisco Bay. In this scene, Mount Diablo is visible in the distance across the bay.

The Lewis and Clark expedition is America's greatest adventure story. The journals kept by the two leaders and some of the men are filled with incidents of great courage and danger, considerable mystery, and continuous suspense. The only heroine, a sixteen-year-old Shoshone named Sacagawea, joined the explorers near the Mandan villages where they camped for the winter. Sacagawea, or Bird Woman, was the consort of Charbonneau, a French trader who had bought her from the Hidatsa, who had captured her during a raid on the Shoshones.

When Lewis and Clark learned from Sacagawea that they would need horses to cross the Rockies, and that the only source of horses was her people, the Shoshones, the explorers quickly employed her as a guide and interpreter. They had to pay the lazy Charbonneau to accompany her. On April 7, 1805, they began the next stage of the journey, upriver into country where, as Lewis stated in his journal, "the foot of civilized man had never trodden."

The meeting with the Shoshones was one of the most dramatic events of the journey. On August 13, Lewis and three of his men stumbled upon three women, who were frightened until Drouillard, the interpreter, soothed them with signs, a few words, and presents. Lewis asked the women to take them to the Shoshone camp. As he and the men followed the women down a trail into an open area, they were confronted by about sixty mounted warriors galloping in a wild charge to rescue their women.

Unfortunately, at that moment Sacagawea was miles away with Clark's party of searchers, but fortunately one of the women they had treated kindly shouted to the warriors that these were friendly strangers, and she held up one of the presents they had given her. To Lewis's surprise, the Shoshone chief dismounted, embraced Lewis, and said in Shoshone: "I am pleased! I am much rejoiced!" Later, the reunion of Sacagawea with her people was an occasion for an evening of celebration, with much dancing and singing.

After trading goods for twenty-eight horses and one mule, and employing six Shoshone guides, including Sacagawea (who wanted to see the Great Ocean the explorers constantly spoke of), they began the arduous climb over the last ranges. They spent the month of October in a race to reach the Pacific before winter overtook them. On the morning of November 7, the Columbia River was shrouded in fog. Gradually the air cleared and they saw ahead of them the blue of the Pacific. "Ocean in view!" Clark scribbled in his logbook. "O! the joy."

At the end of 4,100 miles, they spent the winter on high ground near a river now called the Lewis and Clark. The return journey to St. Louis, beginning March 23, 1806, and ending September 23, was not easy, but everyone survived, completing one of the world's greatest true adventures.

During the period that followed the Spaniards' venture into the Southwest, the British and the European nations continued to establish colonies between the Atlantic shore and the Mississippi River. Then, after years of contention with England, the United States of America was created. In 1803, when the French let it be known that they needed cash more than their land in North America, President Thomas Jefferson seized the opportunity to buy half a billion acres for less than three cents per acre, thus doubling the size of the country. Almost as soon as the Louisiana Purchase was ratified, President Jefferson began planning an exploration of the territory. Meriwether Lewis and William Clark led the expedition to the Pacific Coast. They and several of their men kept written accounts of the events. This journey through unknown and unmapped lands was an epic adventure filled with danger, mystery, and continuous suspense.

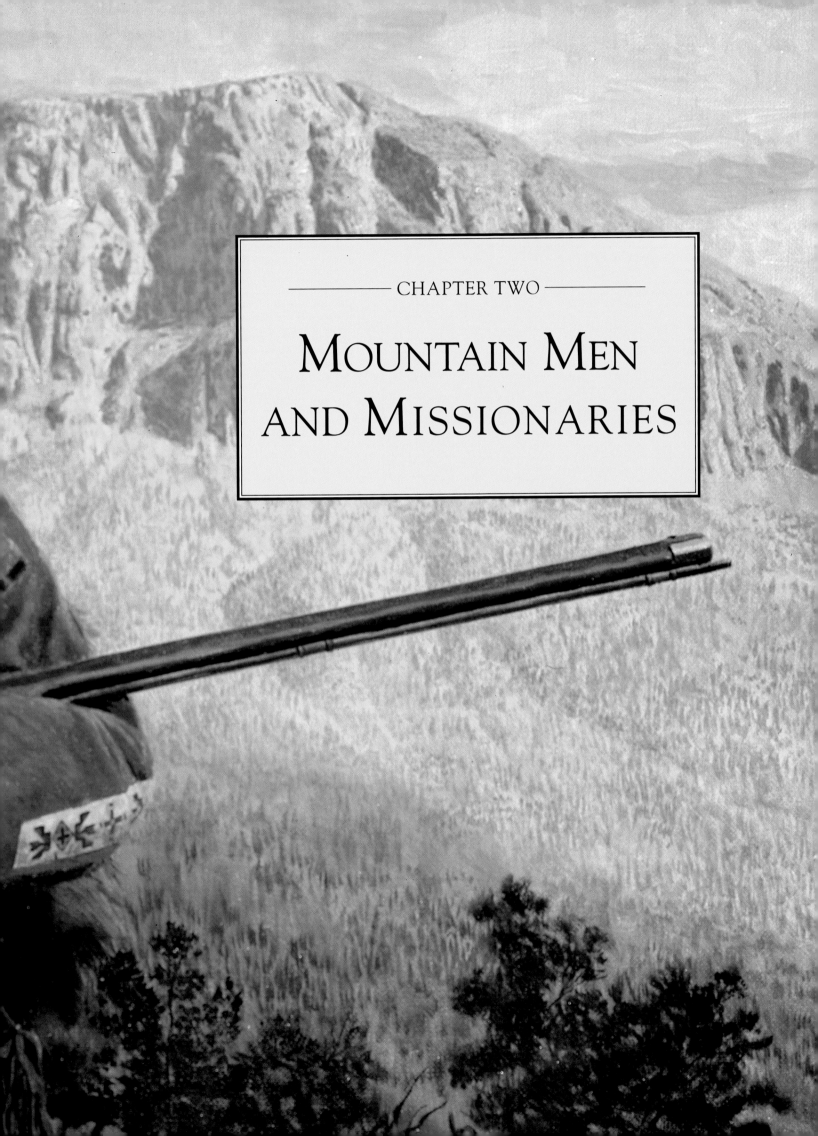

CHAPTER TWO

MOUNTAIN MEN AND MISSIONARIES

Early in the nineteenth century, St. Louis, a city growing prosperous from the fur trade, considered itself to be "the capital of the West." On August 21, 1813, Auguste Chouteau, above, read an announcement of the charter for the first bank in Missouri Territory. Standing beside him on the porch of the Laclede-Chouteau House was Manuel Lisa who, with Chouteau, dominated the fur trade in those early years. Among those present was also Governor William Clark, explorer of the West.

While the Lewis and Clark explorers were returning down the Missouri River, they met two young men on August 26, 1806, paddling upriver in a canoe. They were from Illinois, traveling west in hopes of making their fortunes by trapping beavers. In those early years of the nineteenth century, hatters and coat makers around the world were crying for more beaver pelts. European armies wanted tricorn beaver hats, working men wanted broad-brimmed beaver hats, rich dandies demanded high-crowned beaver hats. The Hudson's Bay Company in Canada could not supply the demand, and numerous young American frontiersmen were venturing into their nation's newly acquired territory in pursuit of pelts.

John Colter, one of the soldiers with Lewis and Clark, had trapped a few beavers whenever the expedition halted for any length of time, and after he spoke with the two young men, they invited him to join them. Colter immediately asked Clark for a discharge, which was granted, and off he went back west with his new friends in search of fortune.

In the spring of 1807 after a fairly successful season, Colter packed his beaver pelts in a canoe and started down the Missouri eager to see St. Louis and civilization after an absence of three years. Near the mouth of the Platte, he met a keelboat loaded with forty-two men led by Manuel Lisa, organizer of the new Missouri Fur Company. George Drouillard, Colter's friend of the Lewis and Clark expedition, was aboard and he and Lisa persuaded Colter to join their company and return to the Rockies.

Colter agreed to join the Missouri Fur Company at a time when fur trading was swiftly becoming an international contest for control of a high-finance business. British, Scottish, and American companies set trappers against trappers, and tribes against tribes. The Blackfeet worked and fought for the British, the Crows for the Americans. John Colter was soon caught up in this rivalry. The Blackfeet captured him twice, and he escaped twice, but the third time they stripped him naked and told him that if he could outrun them, they would spare his life. Colter won the race, creating one of the great folk legends of the West. But at the first opportunity after that, he returned to St. Louis vowing never to set foot in the wilderness again.

In 1821 two large Canada-based fur companies, the North West and Hudson's Bay, became one mighty corporation and began sending their trappers farther and farther south into United States territory. American interests finally persuaded the government to send military protection, and in 1822 William H. Ashley and Andrew Henry, manufacturers of gunpowder and lead near St. Louis, ventured into the fur business.

Advertising in St. Louis newspapers, they brought together a remarkable group of bold frontiersmen. TO ENTERPRISING YOUNG MEN, the advertisement began, and went on to seek the services of one hundred men to ascend the Missouri River to its source, and there to be employed for one, two, or three years.

Among those given employment were Thomas Fitzpatrick, sixteen-year-old James Bridger, thirty-year-old James Clyman, former pirate High Glass, the mythic fifty-two-year-old Mike Fink, and probably most remarkable of all, Jedediah Smith. Smith was twenty-three years old; he had read reports of the Lewis and Clark expedition and was eager to see that newly explored territory. Eventually Smith and his companions were to become known as the Mountain Men. Their courage and energy would play a considerable role in the United States' acquisition of California and the Oregon Territory.

Nine years after Chouteau's announcement of the bank charter, William Ashley and Andrew Henry entered the fur trade, employing a small army of frontiersmen to venture into the Rocky Mountains in search of beaver pelts. Out of Ashley's and Henry's imaginative endeavors came the legendary Mountain Men of the fur trade. Among these trappers, explorers, and trailblazers were men whose names are now imprinted upon the West—Jim Bridger, Thomas Fitzpatrick, John Colter, James Clyman, and the great mapmaker Jedediah Smith.

The Mountain Men learned early that successful beaver trappers had to wade in icy water for hours so they would leave no scent, that they could not survive unless they learned everything that the Indians knew, that they must learn to read the meanings of every sound, every turned leaf, broken twig, or sudden flight of birds, every manifestation of the natural world around them.

Ashley and Henry soon abandoned the old fixed trading post method used by their predecessors and rivals. They introduced the annual rendezvous. When each trapper went out in winter he was informed of the time, usually in June, and the place, a carefully selected site often somewhere in what is now western Wyoming. The rendezvous site chosen had to offer plentiful grass and water for the hundreds of horses that would bring in the participants. Trade goods to exchange for pelts were brought on schedule from St. Louis. Whiskey was in plentiful supply. Trappers, traders, and entire Indian families from tepee villages near and far came to celebrate in these summer fairs. "A species of Saturnalia," an observer reported in his description of the feasting, drinking, gambling, horse racing, shooting matches, and buffalo chases.

Jedediah Smith and Jim Bridger were among the Mountain Men who ventured into areas that later became states of the Far West. From a Crow Indian, Smith learned of the South Pass route around the Wind River mountains and over the Continental Divide. In only one generation this would be a crowded gateway to Oregon and California. Smith mapped large areas for the first time, and he and his companions helped to bring the richness of these untrodden

regions, an agrarian paradise, into the consciousness of the nation.

Late in the 1830s the demand for beaver pelts began to diminish. The last great rendezvous was held in 1840. The following year, May 1841, a pioneer band of seventy men, women, and children left Independence, Missouri, bound for the Far West with the intention of settling somewhere there forever.

The fourteen wagons and seventy persons leaving Independence in 1841 were a mixed bag of emigrants that included veteran Mountain Man Thomas Fitzpatrick as guide, Father Pierre-Jean De Smet, two other Catholic priests, and a Methodist minister, the Reverend Joseph Williams. It was the first wagon train to travel all the way to the Pacific. Converting Indians to Christianity was a motivating force for many of those Oregon-bound pilgrims. Marcus Whitman, a physician and ardent Presbyterian, had preceded them five years earlier, traveling with a fur trapping expedition, to establish Whitman Mission, which was already attracting visionaries in the East.

In 1842 a larger group, about one hundred people in eighteen wagons, undertook a similar journey. In 1843 Marcus Whitman organized his Great Migration of families numbering a thousand persons, traveling in a hundred wagons with five thousand head of livestock. Two years later, three thousand more made the journey, and in 1847 five thousand. Of these ventures Horace Greeley, the famous newspaper editor, was intensely critical, describing them as "foolhardy," and their venture as "palpable homicide" and "insanity" and predicting that nine-tenths of the travelers would not reach the Columbia River alive. A few years later, however, Greeley changed his mind and in his editorials was advising: "Go West, young man."

After abandoning the old custom of fixed trading posts where trappers brought their packs of pelts, the fur companies held an annual rendezvous in early summer. Trade goods from St. Louis were exchanged for furs. Trappers, traders, and Indians feasted and celebrated together in what some observers described as a "bacchanal." In this scene a tomahawk-throwing contest is under way.

The route these hardy overlanders followed had been laid out by the Mountain Men. Leaving Independence or Westport the wagon trains followed the old Santa Fe Trail for a short distance, then crossed the Kansas River and headed northwestward for Fort Kearny on the Platte River. As the flow of emigrants increased, Fort Kearny quickly grew from a single blockhouse to a major military post. From Kearny the trail led along the Platte to Fort Laramie at the juncture of the North Platte and Laramie rivers. Founded in 1834 as a supply base for fur trappers, Fort Laramie soon became an oasis for overland travelers. Within the safety of the fort they could repair wagons, replenish supplies, rest and recruit livestock, wash clothes, and bathe in the river. And for many it was a first close encounter with Indians, who also came to the fort to trade.

While the emigrants were on the trail the sudden appearance of mounted warriors some yards distant was startling, even frightening, but in and around the fort they found these native people fascinating. The easterners admired the colorful dress and ornaments of the men and the women and were eager to trade. "For a piece of chewing tobacco as big as a hand," a traveler noted, "one could get a fine buffalo hide. Some Indians would sell everything they had on."

During the early years at Fort Laramie unofficial records were kept of passing travelers. After the U.S. Army took over, efforts were made to keep an exact count. A table of emigrant and Indian deaths on the trail is quite revealing. In 1841 one Indian was reported killed by emigrants on the Oregon Trail. In 1845 it was four emigrants and one Indian, and in 1846, four emigrants, twenty Indians. The numbers on both sides would sharply increase during the high traffic of the Gold Rush period.

For a wagon train to make a successful crossing, advance planning and organization were necessary. A company would be formed with laws and bylaws drawn to establish rules. A captain and other officers would be chosen by vote. Punishments for infractions of rules were named. Decisions by the majority were as rigid as law. When James Reed of the ill-fated Donner party, for example, killed a fellow member he was banished from the train although he pleaded self-defense. If a veteran fur trapper was available he would be employed as a guide.

After leaving Fort Laramie the wagons followed the North Platte westward, passed Independence Rock, and crossed the Continental Divide through the famous South Pass that had been discovered by the Mountain Men. This gateway to Oregon and California was twenty miles wide, rising gradually and offering no spectacular vistas. Until more direct cutoffs were mapped, the emigrants then turned southwestward to Jim Bridger's fort on Green River, and then northwestward to Fort Hall. The most difficult part of the two-thousand-mile journey to Oregon was now behind them. In a few weeks the average six-month trek would be ended.

The home on wheels in which the overlanders traveled was originally the old reliable Conestoga, a wagon created in the valley of that name in Lancaster County, Pennsylvania. Conestogas were hauling freight in the eastern colonies half a century before the Revolutionary War, and they were brought early to the Missouri staging towns for western crossings. Because Conestogas were built for hauling freight instead of humans, changes were gradually made and they became Prairie Schooners. Yet they were still basically Conestogas, with undercurve beds and overhanging ends that gave them the appearance of high-prowed boats being towed by six horses or mules or oxen.

In the 1840s, as the fur trade began to wane, missionaries and prospective settlers ventured into the West. In the spring of 1841, seventy men, women, and children left Independence, Missouri, bound for the Far West. This was the first wagon train to travel all the way from Missouri to the Pacific. The route they followed had been laid out by Mountain Men.

Because their undercurve beds and overhanging ends gave them the appearance of boats, the Conestoga wagons that were used on the westward crossings were called Prairie Schooners.

One of the wonders of the Prairie Schooner was the canvas covers, supported by eight to sixteen bows. When a severe thunderstorm struck a wagon near Fort Kearny, one woman inside later said that the wind rocked the wagon furiously and "the rain turned to hail and blew and beat against the canvas, but we didn't get wet." The cloth used for covered wagons was Osnaburg, spun of hemp and flax and originally imported from Germany. Raindrops bounced off it.

As a journey progressed, the interior of a Prairie Schooner became a woman's province. Wives and daughters were forced to adjust to a radically changed environment, but the duties were similar to those they had left back home. Food had to be cooked, clothes mended and laundered, children tended. One woman diarist wrote that she and her husband had a straw bed, a featherbed, pillows, one sheet, and two blankets. Trunks and boxes down the middle of the wagon provided privacy for them and their two daughters, who occupied the opposite bed.

Most of the cooking was done during the evening, when the train usually formed a circle as it halted for the night. The enclosed circle was not especially meant for protection from Indian attack, but to keep the cattle and unharnessed draft animals secure and to provide places for cooking fires. Common fare consisted of boiled potatoes, batches of saleratus biscuits, dried beans and apples and peaches, and slices of very salty side bacon. Because of its keeping qualities rice increased in popularity on the trail.

At first daylight the wagons and their occupants were expected to be ready to roll. The last act after hitching animals was to count children. Shortly before noon the train would be halted again, near a stream if possible. This midday stop, usually for two hours, was called "nooning." The animals were fed and watered and the overlanders would likely eat leftovers instead of cooking.

At day's end, the women prepared food for their families. The cooking was usually done within a circle of wagons that was intended to keep cattle and unharnessed draft animals secure, rather than as a protection against very rare Indian attacks.

Because most wagon trains left for Oregon or California in early spring, they crossed the Plains and entered the Rockies during the time of the West's greatest display of floral beauty. Many letter writers commented upon the richness of colors. One compared the adorned earth to a Persian rug of lavender, red, and yellow mixed with silver green prairie grass.

The writers commented upon the draft animals that took on personalities during their close relationship over many weeks. Some said that mules moved at a more gentle pace than horses. Others admired the oxen because they walked with a slow rhythm that swayed the wagons so slightly that it was possible to read or write while seated inside.

Passage to Oregon or California by wagon train was an experience never forgotten. One overlander told of the slow progress—fifteen to twenty miles a day across the Plains, even less in the mountains. "We traveled many a weary mile," another complained, and then declared: "But there were many things to laugh about."

Women worked hard to maintain the homes on wheels in which the overlanders traveled, and they looked forward to a few minutes of recreation during the daily "noonings" when the wagon trains halted to rest and water the teams. Most trains traveled in the spring and summer when wildflowers carpeted the immense plains.

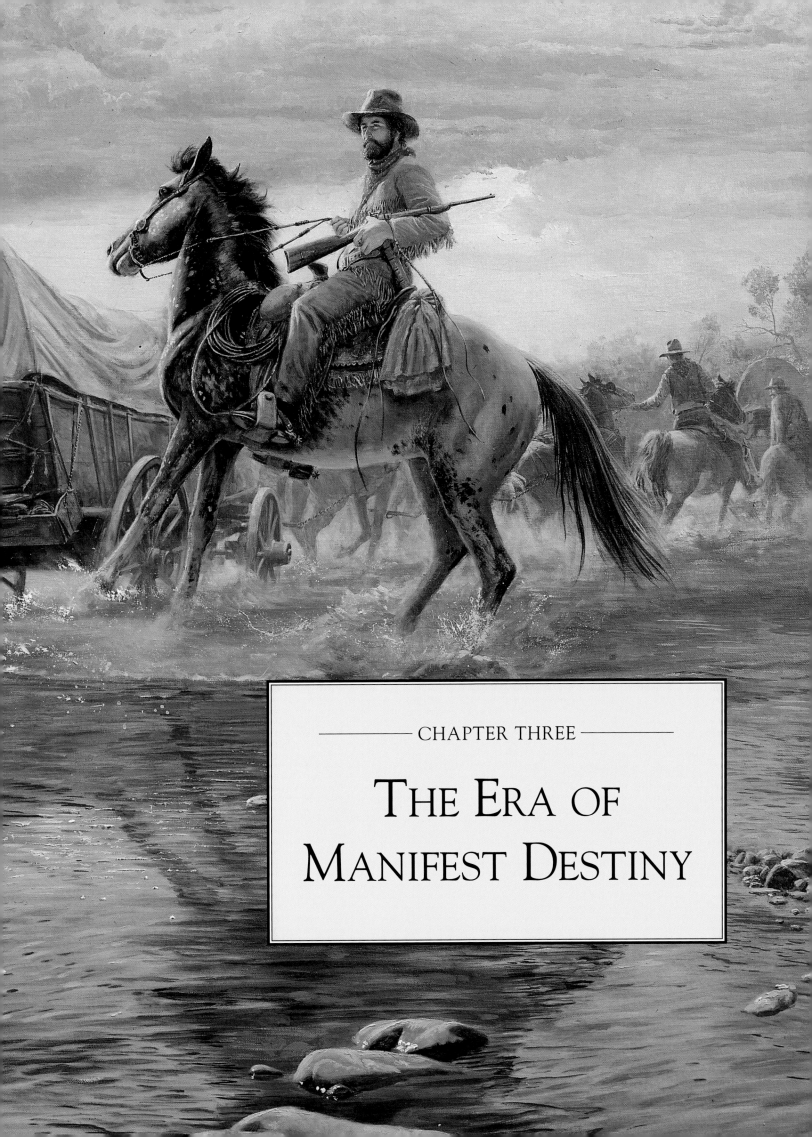

CHAPTER THREE

THE ERA OF
MANIFEST DESTINY

In December of 1845, a New York lawyer and journalist put the words "manifest" and "destiny" together in a sentence and thus created a slogan that suited the mood of millions of Americans of that time: "The fulfillment of our manifest destiny to overspread the continent allotted by Providence," John O'Sullivan wrote. For many years into the future, Manifest Destiny would be the godlike justification for rapid settlement of the West, for the conquest of the Indian tribes and the taking of the vast lands they occupied.

In the 1840s the slogan supported the stratagem for adding the Oregon Territory to the United States, annexing Texas, and fighting a war with Mexico for California and the Southwest.

The Santa Fe Trail played as large a part in the acquisition of the Southwest as the Oregon Trail played in the Northwest. Twenty years before wagon trains were traveling to Oregon, venturesome trappers and traders were prowling the Arkansas River country and testing the Spanish-owned territory of New Mexico. In 1822 the first freight wagons left the Missouri frontier for Santa Fe: three Conestogas owned by William Becknell.

Becknell's high profits brought numerous other traders into the market and well-defined trails were soon marked out. Travelers on the Santa Fe route faced two obstacles that seldom troubled those on the Oregon Trail. Water was in short supply across many sections and such Indian tribes as the Comanche and Kiowa were more inclined to raid for goods and livestock.

Many wagon trains used forward and flanking scouts to guard against surprise attacks. Wherever there was grass the buffalo thrived, and the herds were often larger than those in the northern plains. The travelers often saw Indian hunters at work. If meat for the trains was in short supply, they would halt long enough to pick off a buffalo or two.

Jedediah Smith—trapper, trader, explorer, and mapmaker—came late to the Santa Fe Trail. After surviving howling blizzards and attacks by Indians and grizzly bears, Smith joined a wagon train that left St. Louis in April 1831. Midway to Santa Fe, while searching for a waterhole on the arid plain below the Arkansas River, he disappeared. Searches by other members of the train proved futile. Not until the wagons reached Santa Fe was the mystery of Smith's disappearance partially solved. A band of Comancheros (Mexicans who traded with Comanches) came in to trade a rifle, a pair of pistols, and other gear that had belonged to Smith. When challenged, they claimed they had bought the articles from Comanches. Exactly how Smith died is not known, but during his thirty-one years he experienced more adventures in the Old West than most men who lived to twice his age.

In 1845, a New York journalist used the phrase "manifest destiny," creating a slogan for the mood of the nation: ". . . our manifest destiny to overspread the continent allotted by Providence." Along the western trails the native peoples watched with awe and apprehension the unending wagon trains rolling across their lands.

Buffalo hunters, like these Crow tribesmen, learned to increase the numbers of their kill by separating a smaller group of animals from the main herd, and then milling them in a circle.

In 1831, the same year that Jedediah Smith disappeared, a young man who had been told by his physician that he was dying of "consumption" joined a train departing Independence, Missouri, for Santa Fe. His name was Josiah Gregg, and he believed that he would die before journey's end. Within a few days, however, the salubrious air, the hard work, and coarse food brought him back to health. After reaching Santa Fe and observing that the owner of the train had made a small fortune, he decided to become a trader himself. Each year for the next eight years he took a train of goods to Santa Fe. In 1843, at the age of thirty-six, he was wealthy enough to retire and write a book about his experiences, *The Commerce of the Prairies*. It was meant for his friends and relatives, but the nationwide interest in the West created such a demand for the book that new editions had to be printed in rapid succession. After one hundred and fifty years it is still in print, a classic work on Santa Fe trade and the wagon trains that made it possible.

By 1846 the nation was imbued with expansionism. The fall of the Alamo ten years earlier had only spurred the determination of Texas pioneers to continue their fight for independence. In 1845, the United States annexed Texas, and this inevitably led to the war with Mexico that began on May 12, 1846.

On June 9, a well-to-do Santa Fe trader named Samuel Magoffin left Independence, Missouri, on a secret mission for President James Polk. Oregon had been gained without force, and the United States government was hopeful that New Mexico and California could be brought into the Union through negotiations. Magoffin had close ties with Mexican officials and was being sent to Santa Fe to pave the way for General Stephen Kearny's Army of the West. Kearny hoped to capture Santa Fe without resorting to arms.

Kearny's army was in motion early in June, leaving Fort Leavenworth in sections, interspersed with supply wagons. Except for one regiment of regular army infantry the soldiers were mostly volunteers. The nation had not been to war for thirty years, and as usually happens after long periods of peace, the U.S. Congress had allowed the military to languish. What trained forces existed were mainly in the Army of the Rio Grande, under the command of General Zachary Taylor. Consequently Kearny was desperate for volunteers from the frontier states to fill his ranks. He discovered that hundreds of young men adhering to the faith of the Latter Day Saints were camped along the Missouri River awaiting orders from Brigham Young, the Mormon leader, to start trekking west.

When Kearny offered to enlist five hundred of these Mormons, Brigham Young was delighted. He had almost no money to finance the first wagon trains to the West to settle his people permanently, and he was sure that the men enlisting would send most of their pay to their families and church. Also, the men who marched as soldiers to Santa Fe would be fed and clothed and end their enlistment somewhere near the new Mormon homeland. Since Young hoped to settle his people somewhere in territory claimed by Mexico, he was very much in favor of the acquisition of the Southwest by the United States.

In the 1840s the trail to Santa Fe became as busy as the trail to Oregon and California. Overland traders were soon joined by General Kearny's Army of the West.

In Texas, Americans opposed to Mexican rule fought Santa Anna at the Alamo. Although most of the Texas defenders died there, a month later the independent Republic of Texas was created, eventually to become one of the United States.

The result was the formation of the Mormon Battalion, which was attached to Kearny's Army of the West for the long march to Santa Fe. Traveling a few days ahead of the army were Samuel Magoffin and his spirited eighteen-year-old wife, Susan. Although Samuel was more than twice Susan's age, they were a romantic couple and she was already pregnant. For the long overland journey, Samuel luxuriously outfitted a closed carriage. It was cushioned with pillows and provided with books, medicines, and the feminine necessities of the time. One of Susan's favorite books was Josiah Gregg's *The Commerce of the Prairies*. She used it as a guidebook, and when writing in her diary she sometimes adopted the author's style.

On July 8, a company of Kearny's soldiers overtook the Magoffin train, and Samuel received orders to proceed to Bent's Fort and await the arrival of his brother James and General Kearny.

According to legend, James was carrying a satchel filled with gold coins, presumably for use in the occupation of Santa Fe. On July 26, Samuel and Susan reached Bent's Fort, where Susan fell ill and suffered a miscarriage. While she was recovering, James Magoffin and General Kearny arrived. Busy though they were with plans to capture Santa Fe, both men called upon Susan to wish her well.

Not until a week later was she able to travel on the crowded trail to Santa Fe. Meanwhile, General Kearny had issued a proclamation to the citizens of New Mexico, informing them that a great military force was approaching "to ameliorate their condition" and to seek their union with the United States. To the governor of New Mexico at Santa Fe, the general dispatched a letter informing him that the Rio Grande from its source to the delta was now the boundary between the United States and Mexico.

Reinforced by the volunteer Mormon Battalion, the Army of the West moved on to Santa Fe, capturing the old Spanish city without firing a shot.

In California, General John C. Fremont solidified opposition to Mexican control, and another western state was soon added to the Union.

On August 18, General Kearny and a company of dragoons marched into the plaza at Santa Fe to discover that the governor had departed. Without firing a shot, the Army of the West added the territories of New Mexico and what is now Arizona to the Union. A few days later the Magoffins arrived and Susan recorded in her diary that they celebrated with oysters and champagne. In the meantime, far to the east General Zachary Taylor's Army of the Rio Grande had crossed that newly proclaimed border of the United States, drawing off the forces of Mexico from Santa Fe and the Southwest.

While these momentous events were occurring in New Mexico, Lieutenant Archibald Gillespie of the U.S. Marines was acting as a secret agent for President Polk on the Pacific Coast. His primary mission was to find General John C. Fremont and persuade him to return to California from Oregon, where the Mexican governor had banished him for seditionary activities. Although Fremont knew his life would be in danger, the assured support from his government led him to return with Gillespie as far as Sutter's Fort. There he found a band of trappers, hunters, and probably a few outlaws. This motley force stole a herd of horses from Mexican soldiers and captured a retired colonel, Mariano Vallejo, in Sonoma. They took him and his family to Sutter's Fort to be imprisoned.

At Sonoma, the rebels proclaimed themselves a republic, and made a flag from a bedsheet. In one corner they painted a red star facing a crudely drawn bear. With black paint they fashioned the words "California Republic." To this day these symbols remain part of the flag of the State of California.

Fremont, with Lieutenant Gillespie acting as his adjutant, now took command of the guerrilla band. They marched triumphantly to San Francisco and seized the presidio without firing a shot. On July 4, they celebrated the birth of the California Republic. Three days later, however, Commodore John D. Sloat, commanding a small fleet off Monterey, landed a force of two hundred and fifty men. After running up a flag over the customhouse, in accordance with his orders, the commodore began acting as if he had raised the Stars and Stripes over the whole of California. He sent a small force to Sonoma and seized the Bear Flag capital in the name of the United States. And so ended the brief lifetime of the Republic of California.

In September, General Kearny, who was in Santa Fe, prepared an expedition to join in the conquest of California. By mid-October the Mormon Battalion was marched to San Diego. They were dependent largely upon mules and wagons for transport, and were constantly short of rations. After crossing deserts, cactus thickets, unmarked boulder-strewn passages, and difficult rivers, they reached San Diego at the end of January 1847. Virtually all military action had ceased in southern California, but the Mormons still had five months of enlisted service and they needed pay to send to their families whenever they reached their permanent home in the West. Because of lack of communications, members of the Mormon Battalion still did not know what part of the West Brigham Young had chosen for the Latter-Day Saints.

Back along the Missouri River in Iowa and Nebraska, Young and his followers had spent a difficult winter, and it was not until midsummer of 1847 that the Mormons brought together a train of seventy-two wagons for a journey into the West. Young and his apostles had decided upon the type of area in which they wanted to settle and the general location, but not the exact place. Many wanted to go all the way to California, but legend has it that when Young first looked down into the valley of the Salt Lake, in what is now Utah, he declared: "This is the place."

Four more wagon trains crossed the Plains during the summer of 1847. Thousands of Mormons were still camped along the Missouri River and farther east. All were eager to make the crossing and lend their efforts to planting crops, digging irrigation ditches, and building homes and roads in the land they now called Deseret.

To inspire safety the Mormons built their first houses like forts, with doors and windows facing an interior center, the rear walls left solid except for loopholes for defense.

The following spring they planted five thousand acres, mostly of wheat. But as the grain began to ripen, swarms of giant crickets attacked the crop. The Mormons fought back with sticks, boards, and rags. They were losing the battle until a flock of seagulls flew in from the Great Salt Lake. The gulls devoured the crickets and saved the wheat crop, which is the reason the seagull is the state bird of Utah and there is a monument in Salt Lake City to honor the seagull.

During the following decade the Mormons endured many more ordeals, particularly in crossings of the Plains and the Rockies, but they persevered. Like other settlers in the early years of the West, they were convinced that Manifest Destiny was ordained by Providence and that it was their duty to take what lands were necessary for them to prosper.

And so it was during a few months in the years 1846 and 1847 that the people of the United States claimed an enormous spread of Western America—California, and New Mexico, and Arizona. With the winning of the war with Mexico, Texas was now secure as a part of the Union. And the Mormons were settling Deseret, which would become Utah, yet another state in the Union.

With the immense Northwest now part of the United States, settlers from the East came to establish farms and ranches. Here a family is getting ready to celebrate its first Christmas in the new land.

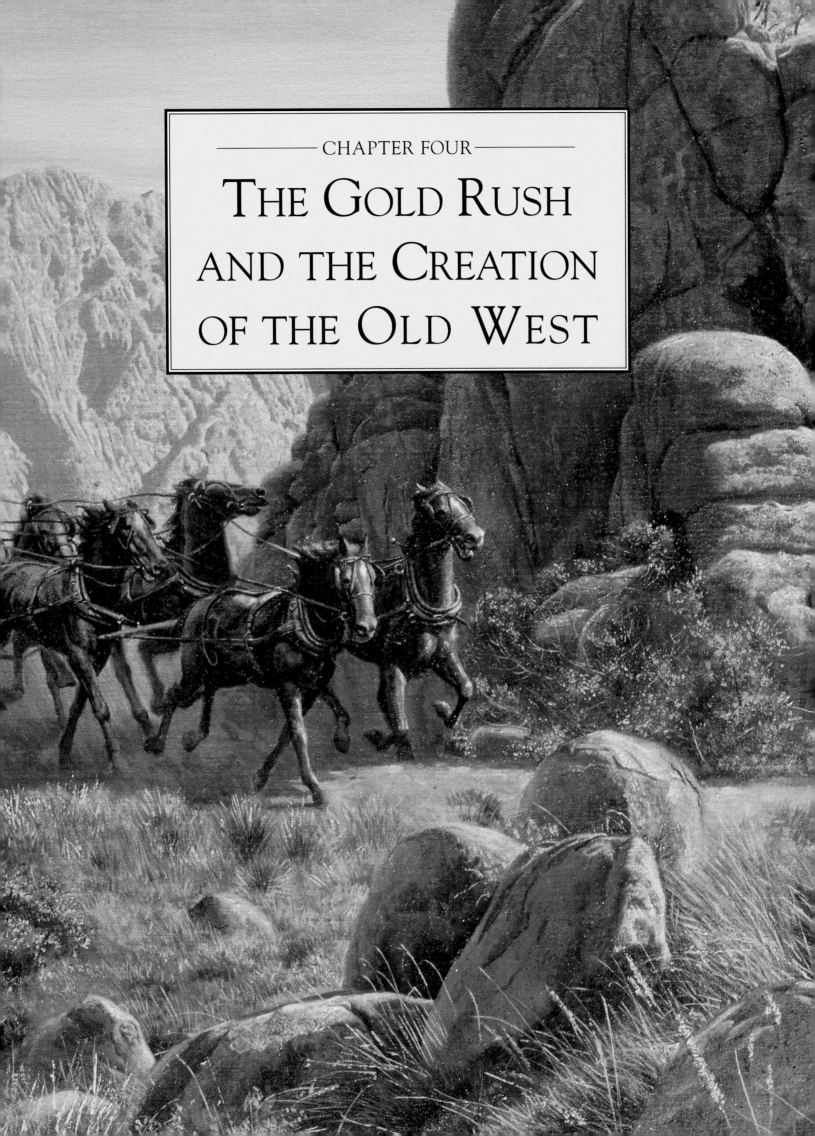

CHAPTER FOUR

THE GOLD RUSH
AND THE CREATION
OF THE OLD WEST

On January 24, 1848, James Marshall, a carpenter, discovered gold on the south fork of California's American River. He and his employer, John Sutter, were unable to keep the find a secret, and from that day everything was changed in the West. As soon as the news spread, thousands of Californians descended upon the area.

After soldiers of the Mormon Battalion completed the terms of their enlistments, nine of them made their way north to Sutter's Fort, where they found employment. One of them, Henry Bigler, was to be present at one of the most consequential events in the history of the American West.

John Augustus Sutter was an adventurous man whose ambition had no boundaries, who took great risks, and whose fortunes rose and fell. He left his native Switzerland in 1834 and upon arrival in New York headed for the frontier, hoping to find a fortune. In St. Louis he bought a wagonload of cheap goods from pawnshops, joined a train bound for Santa Fe, and made a grand stake. Four years later he was in California, bargaining with the Mexican government for a land grant.

Sutter's land grant at the junction of the Sacramento and American rivers consisted of about fifty thousand acres. He named it New Helvetia. From a departing colony of Russians he made a credit deal for hundreds of cattle, sheep, and horses; agricultural implements; and an arsenal of French weapons the Russians had captured from Napoleon. Sutter built a fort with twenty-four French guns mounted on the ramparts. By the time Henry Bigler and other members of the Mormon Battalion arrived, a ranch house, workshops, and mills were completed or under construction. Bigler was assigned to work for James Marshall, Sutter's carpenter, who was building a sawmill on the south fork of the American River.

On January 24, 1848, Bigler (who was a poor speller) noted in his diary: "This day some kind of mettle was found in the tail race that looks like goald. first discovered by James Martial, the Boss of the Mill." This brief entry was the first written record of the forthcoming Gold Rush.

Six days later, Bigler made another entry: "Our metal has been tride and prooves to be goald."

During that six-day interval, Marshall had taken the flakes and granules down to the fort to show Sutter. Neither man knew how to test for gold, but Sutter owned an encyclopedia that contained instructions, which they followed until they were certain that the metal Marshall had found was indeed gold. (This occurrence makes one wonder—if Sutter had not owned the encyclopedia, how long would the world have waited for a discovery that changed everything in the Old West?)

Sutter tried to keep the gold a secret, but his entire kingdom of New Helvetia knew all about it within a week. By early spring the little port town of San Francisco was astir with rumors of fortunes to be found around Sutter's Fort. A few weeks later, a hired messenger brought several specimens of gold to the Reverend Walter Colton in Monterey. As soon as the news spread through the town, Colton wrote, "The blacksmith dropped his hammer, the carpenter his plane, the mason his trowel, the farmer his sickle, the baker his loaf, and the tapster his bottle. All were off for the mines, some on horses, some on carts, and some on crutches, and one went in a litter."

Within a few months, forty percent of the enlisted men stationed in California deserted to dig for gold, and quite often the soldiers sent to arrest the deserters also joined the gold hunters.

Back in the eastern states, however, the general public was skeptical at first. But then, in December, specimens of California gold reached Washington. In a message to Congress, President Polk transformed the gold-strike stories from rumor to fact. Before the December holidays ended, thousands of easterners were

preparing to go in search of fortunes in gold. Eighty thousand traveled to California in 1849—the 49ers—some by ship around Cape Horn, but most went overland, following the old Oregon Trail. Less than five thousand of the travelers were women and children. The seventy-five thousand males were a rowdy bunch of argonauts. Fearing the Indians, they went well armed. The number of Indians reported killed by overlanders in 1848 was two; in 1849 the number rose to sixty. Unlike the Oregon-bound families of previous years, few of the "Forty-niners" considered themselves emigrants. They were going to the gold fields to get rich and they planned to return home. From what they had heard and read, most believed they could find a fortune in a few weeks, or months, no more than a year. A single large nugget would make it possible for them to return home very rich, they thought.

At Sutter's Fort, meanwhile, mobs of gold seekers intruded upon the owner's lands. They slaughtered Sutter's livestock, trampled his fields, and even stole the French cannons from his fort. Some of his workmen joined the prospectors; others fled. The corrupt local courts declared his land title invalid and the invaders quickly divided New Helvetia into gold claims. Thirty years later Sutter died broke in a shabby hotel in Washington, still beseeching the government to return his stolen lands.

The offensive treasure hunters sought out James Marshall because he had been the first to find gold. They stole his horses, his food, and his mining tools. When he tried to drive them away, they hired armed guards to keep him off his own property. When he went to court, he found the prejudiced jury allied with the trespassers. His own lawyer was paid off by them.

When Marshall tried to travel in search of a distant prospecting site, some of his tormentors followed him, believing that he could find gold by divination. Everywhere that he stopped to dig or pan, a small army surrounded him, threatening to hang him unless he found another rich lode for them. Finally Marshall gave up and returned to Coloma, near where he had found the first gold, and began making his living working at odd jobs. Thirty-five years later he died penniless.

Finding gold or silver in the Old West seldom put the discoverers on the road to permanent wealth. In Nevada in 1857 Peter O'Riley and Pat McLaughlin, a pair of impecunious Irishmen, were digging a ditch to collect water for rocker mining. While they were at work Henry T. P. Comstock, a fellow miner, happened along and saw flashes of gold in the gravel. He immediately pronounced himself their partner.

From the eastern United States, multitudes of treasure hunters sought a way to the West. Thousands traveled overland; others braved the rough seas around Cape Horn to San Francisco.

The famous Comstock Lode, which made Virginia City a boomtown, was named for him. For a time the three partners were immensely wealthy, but this did not last. Peter O'Riley died penniless in an insane asylum. Patrick McLaughlin tried to double his fortune by buying mining stock. He ended his days in poverty, working as a mining camp cook. As for H. T. P. Comstock, he gave most of his fortune away, and when he tried to recoup in Montana, he failed and committed suicide.

Bill Fairweather found what he called a "scad" of gold at Alder Gulch, Montana, on May 26, 1863. Within a few weeks, ten thousand prospectors arrived to create another Virginia City. Bill Fairweather delighted in finding gold, caring little about keeping it or buying things with it. He gave most of it away to children. When he died at thirty-nine, his friends buried him in the town's Boothill Cemetery.

Ed Schieffelen made a fabulous silver strike in 1877 and founded the town of Tombstone in Arizona. Schieffelen lived well for several years, enjoying San Francisco's high society. When the money ran out he tried prospecting in Alaska, but had no luck. He was digging in Oregon at the time of a fatal heart attack. Schieffelen left enough funds to pay for his burial atop the granite hills that look down on old Tombstone.

One of the devastating effects of gold and silver strikes, especially in California, was the virtual destruction of numerous tribes of Indians. These events went almost unnoticed in the press, pulpit, or government agencies. More than anywhere else in the West, the natives who lived in areas of rich pay dirt were regarded as superfluous beings, hindrances that must be put out of the way of superior beings. Estimates indicate that as many as nine out of ten of the tribes inhabiting California mining areas were gone by the end of the gold rush—from disease or deliberate extermination.

Through the exciting years that followed the discovery of gold in California, lonely prospectors, each equipped with a grubstake, digging tools, and a burro, sought elsewhere for riches in the earth. Virginia City, Alder Gulch, and Tombstone were among the bigger strikes.

As more miners and settlers poured into the West, the demand for swifter communication was met by the Pony Express. Letters were delivered in ten days between Missouri and California. They were carried mostly by teenaged boys, armed and always ready for danger.

In the years between the California gold strike and the Civil War, many eastern Americans were eager to visit the West or to move there to live. Transportation was a major problem, but along the frontier several ingenious men set out to solve it. Among them were three who formed a company that bore their names, William H. Russell, Alexander Majors, and William Waddell. Russell was the guiding genius.

While he was still a teenager, Russell had made his way to Missouri from New England to begin a career in merchandising. By the time he was thirty he was sending wagons to Santa Fe on his own. In those years before railroads were built in the West, the army was in constant need of supplies for its western forts; Russell, Majors, and Waddell was the only firm with enough wagons to fulfill contracts for millions of pounds of needed stores. In addition, merchants in such burgeoning towns as Denver demanded more and more goods that could be transported only by wagons.

"Such acres of wagons," Horace Greeley wrote when he visited the firm's yards in Leavenworth. "No one who does not see can realize how vast a business this is, nor how immense are its outlays as well as income."

The company was soon adding stagecoaches to its freight service, using mail contracts to help pay for the added equipment. And then, in 1860, Russell overcame the opposition of his partners and started the Pony Express. With a mail contract in hand, he built one hundred and ninety stations, ten to fifteen miles apart, between St. Joseph, Missouri, and Sacramento. The postage rate was five dollars per half ounce, which led correspondents to use tissue paper for messages. Newspapers began to print special Pony Express editions on very thin paper. As telegraph lines then ran from most eastern cities to St. Joseph, and from Sacramento to other California cities, the Pony Express became a vital link. Under Russell's close supervision, the Pony Express was soon delivering mail from Missouri to California in about ten days. The eighty riders employed by Russell were mostly teenagers, including one fifteen-year-old orphan who later became known as Buffalo Bill Cody. Cody's friend, Wild Bill Hickok, who weighed more than the top riding limit of one hundred and twenty-five pounds, found employment at one of the stations. Russell's operating procedure was to separate the route into five divisions, each headed by a superintendent who kept close watch over the riders and schedules. Within each division was a series of swing stations and relay stations. The riders began and ended their daily rides at swing, or home, stations. At intervals between the swing stations were relay stations consisting of a shelter, a stable, and perhaps two relay ponies. The home stations were much larger, with bunks and dining facilities.

Although it was organized in great haste and was short-lived, the Pony Express proved to be one of the most dependable mail services ever operated in the United States. Yet it was a financial failure, posting a loss of almost a million dollars.

Russell's chief rival for mail contracts and stage service was John Butterfield, founder of the Overland Mail Company. Butterfield established the longest stagecoach line in the world, from St. Louis to San Francisco, a route of 2,795 miles. To obtain mail and passengers from the southern states, Butterfield added a branch line from Memphis to Fort Smith. On the first run, the *New York Herald* assigned a reporter, Waterman Ormsby, whose dispatches provide a colorful picture of the discomforts, perils, and delights of travel by stagecoach across half of America.

To avoid the winter blizzards of the northern Plains and the Rockies, Butterfield chose a route across Texas and southern New Mexico, following a line of forts built by the army. To cope with rough sections of the road and increase speed, Butterfield devised a new type of coach that he called a Celerity Wagon. It was outfitted with smaller wheels and set close to the road surface. Nine passengers was the limit, sitting three abreast. As the schedule called for travel by

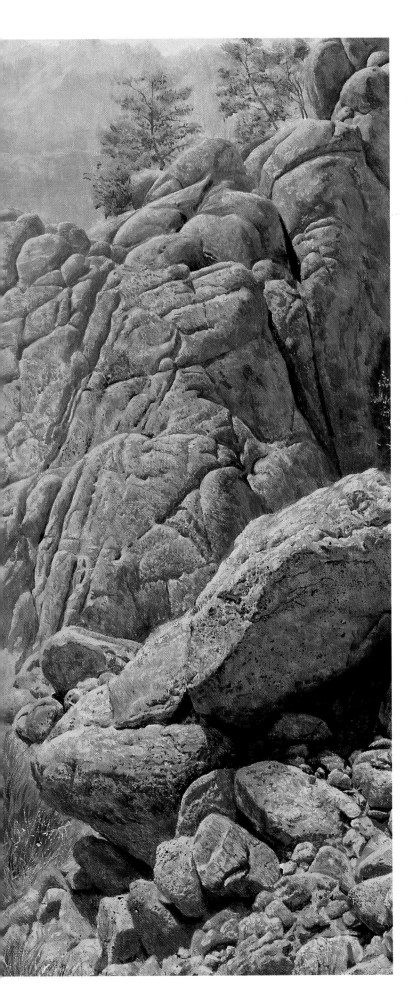

night, the seats were installed so the backs would fold into a single bed for nine passengers. In hilly country the passengers were expected to get out and walk, and sometimes help push the Celerity Wagon over the steeper grades.

Twelve days after leaving St. Louis, reporter Ormsby recorded meeting the first eastbound coach from San Francisco at Guadalupe Pass near El Paso. Both coaches were on schedule for the twenty-five day guarantee of Butterfield's contract. On the first run west, the Celerity Wagon reached San Francisco in twenty-three days, twenty-three and a half hours. Within a year Butterfield's efficient management reduced the time to about twenty-two days, and lowered passenger fares from two hundred dollars to one hundred and fifty. And there was rarely a vacant seat on the Overland Mail Company coaches, bound west or bound east.

Meanwhile, the future of William Russell's Pony Express was under threat from a single wire mounted on poles across the West. Samuel Morse's telegraph, sprung upon the world in 1844, must have been the most rapidly accepted invention of all time. Within ten years virtually all the major cities along the East and West coasts were communicating over telegraph lines. But there was no wire connection between the frontier and the Pacific Coast.

In June 1860 Congress passed the Pacific Telegraph Act and created a fund for subsidizing construction of a line across the West. By late summer Californians were running a line toward Salt Lake City, and the Western Union Telegraph Company sent construction superintendent Edward Creighton westward from Omaha with instructions to string wires to Fort Kearny before winter closed down on his workmen.

Before railroads were built into the West, the transportation of supplies for forts and growing towns required thousands of wagons and draft animals and the hardiest of drivers.

By the following summer, in the first year of the great Civil War, a race was under way between the Californians moving eastward and Creighton's crew moving westward. Creighton's biggest problem was obtaining telegraph poles, which had to be shipped to the treeless Great Plains. In October 1861 the two rivals met in Salt Lake City and the wires were connected.

For delivering a short message the telegraph had no competitors, and a few days later the Pony Express was brought to an end. "Our little friend, the Pony, is to run no more," declared the *Sacramento Bee*. "Farewell and forever, thou staunch, wilderness overcoming, swift-footed messenger."

Outbreak of the Civil War also ended the Overland Mail Company's service over the Butterfield Trail through Confederate Texas, leaving only the weather-threatened Central route available for mail and travelers.

Even greater changes were in store. Although delayed by the war, plans for a transcontinental railroad had been under discussion since the days of the Gold Rush. Beginning in 1853, a series of Pacific Railway surveys undertook to determine the best route from the Mississippi River to the Pacific Ocean. Originally government authorities leaned toward a southern route, but the war soon determined that the first transcontinental railroad would be built along a northern parallel, somewhere along the line of the old Oregon Trail. And the planners, it was soon apparent, would not wait for the war to end before undertaking what some would call "the grandest enterprise under God."

In the Old West, wherever gold moved or moneyed people traveled, the bolder robbers came with their guns.

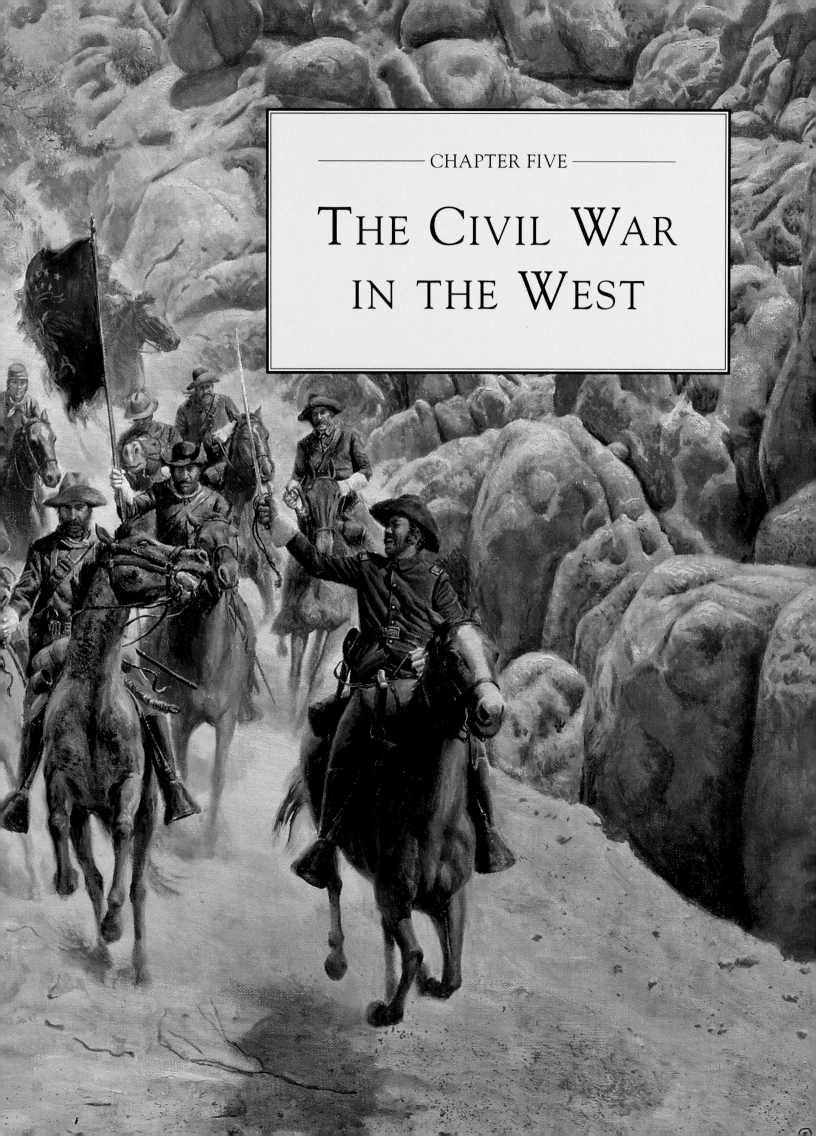

CHAPTER FIVE

THE CIVIL WAR
IN THE WEST

Only three weeks after the Civil War exploded into military action at Bull Run in July 1861, fighting broke out far to the west at Wilson's Creek in Missouri, which was still part of the American frontier. In August a large Confederate army of eleven thousand poorly armed men commanded by General Benjamin McCulloch moved toward Springfield, Missouri, where a better armed Union force, about half that size, was commanded by General Nathaniel Lyon.

The Confederate regiments were originally organized to defend Arkansas and Indian Territory and to hold Missouri as a Confederate state. When General Lyon brought troops west to Springfield, the Confederates decided to attack. The two armies met on August 10 at Wilson's Creek a few miles from Springfield. During fierce fighting General Lyon was killed. The Federals retreated into Springfield, and then east to Rolla, leaving a large part of Missouri under Confederate control.

During the next six months, the Union forces in southwest Missouri were strengthened, and under the command of Samuel Curtis they moved into northwest Arkansas to challenge McCulloch's army. But the Confederates had also grown stronger with fresh soldiers from the tribes of Indian Territory—Cherokees, Creeks, Choctaws, Chickasaws, and Seminoles. President Jefferson Davis sent General Earl Van Dorn to command the Confederates in this important battle.

In the first day of fighting, March 7, 1862, at Pea Ridge (Elkhorn Tavern), Van Dorn surprised Curtis by marching around his position and attacking from the north instead of from the south. The battle was fought fiercely through the day, and the tide seemed to be in the Confederates' favor until Generals McCulloch and McIntosh were killed. Next morning the Federal forces counterattacked and soon drove Van Dorn's regiments from Pea Ridge and into a disastrous retreat toward the Boston Mountains. This battle was the largest fought west of the Mississippi. Its outcome determined that Missouri would remain in the Union. Afterward rumors spread that Indian participants had scalped opponents, but no evidence of this was ever presented.

Meanwhile, in the far Southwest, in territories only recently acquired from Mexico, soldiers of the North and South came to combat in that same year of 1862. Before the battle at Bull Run was fought in Virginia, Colonel John R. Baylor led a Confederate army of twenty-five hundred out of El Paso, with the intention of taking possession of southern New Mexico. Citizens of Tucson and Mesilla leaned toward the Confederacy so that Baylor had little opposition when he declared himself governor. To solidify his claim he sent a delegate to Richmond to represent the territory. Back in Texas during the winter, General Henry H. Sibley was named commander of the Texas forces and soon started a move up the Rio Grande to Santa Fe. The aim was then to proceed northward and seize the Colorado mines.

On February 21,1862, Union General Edward Canby attempted to foil the Confederates' objective by attacking them at Valverde. With little difficulty the Texans drove Canby's men from the field. A month later, however, a regiment of Colorado Volunteers, who had joined the Federals near Santa Fe, added their firepower to a Union force trying to block the Confederates at Pidgeon's Ranch in La Glorieta Pass.

Under Colonel John Slough, the Coloradans held the Texans in the pass on March 26, while a clever flanking movement was undertaken by Major J. M. Chivington and the 1st Colorado Regiment. (Both would become notorious two years later at Sand Creek.) Chivington led a partially mounted force over the

Before the Civil War in the East opened with bloody conflict at Bull Run, forces of the Confederacy and the Union began maneuvering for control of the West. A Confederate army marched out of El Paso, for example, intent upon seizing control of the Southwest. After battles at Valverde and Glorieta Pass, the Confederates were forced to retreat into Texas.

Only three weeks after Bull Run, the first major Civil War battle in the West was fought at Wilson's Creek near Springfield, Missouri. Confederate Colonel James McIntosh, above, led a charge of the Third Louisiana Infantry against a Union battery, an incident that helped turn the battle in the Confederates' favor. A few months later, at Pea Ridge in Arkansas, a Northern army defeated the Southerners and kept Missouri in the Union.

mountains to the rear of the Confederates. To their surprise, from a high ridge the Coloradans looked down upon General Sibley's military supply train, parked and poorly guarded. The Coloradans charged down upon the train, killed or captured its guards, and in short order destroyed the ammunition, rations, and forage, burned the wagons, and slew all the horses.

The fight in the pass continued until both sides withdrew. Meanwhile, small units of loyal Union soldiers were uniting to recapture towns previously taken by the Texans. Sibley soon realized that without supplies the Confederate troops must withdraw into Texas. The retreat was a desperate one, not because of the pursuing enemies, but for lack of food and water. Not until they reached the Rio Grande near Mesilla did they find any relief. At Glorieta Pass dreams of a Southwest Confederacy ended. A few weeks later, Colonel James H. Carleton brought his California Column into New Mexico to make certain that the Confederates would never return.

West of the Mississippi the Confederate forces rarely achieved their objectives, but neither did the Union troops. The real losers in the West were Indian tribes caught up in a conflict that few of them really comprehended.

One of the first individual victims was Cochise, of the Chiricahua Apaches, a tall, broad-shouldered, handsome leader of his people. When the Americans first came to Cochise's Arizona country he welcomed them. He kept his tribesmen from interfering with travelers, and allowed Butterfield's Overland Mail to build a stage station in Apache Pass.

And then in 1861 he was summoned to meet with Lieutenant George Bascom in a tent near the stage station. Believing the meeting would be a social one, Cochise brought along his brother and four other relatives. With scarcely any preliminary remarks, Bascom accused Cochise of stealing the cattle and kidnapping the son of a nearby white rancher. Bascom ordered Cochise to see that the cattle and the boy were returned. Cochise replied truthfully that the Coyoteros from the Gila had done the thieving and kidnapping and that he had no power over them.

Bascom retorted that Cochise was lying and summoned his platoon to surround the tent. At his first opportunity, Cochise knifed a hole in the tent and made his escape in the darkness, but he was fired upon and wounded. His relatives were unable to escape. In an effort to free them, Cochise captured three white men and notified Bascom that he wanted an exchange. Bascom refused, and Cochise executed his prisoners, whereupon Bascom executed Cochise's three male relatives.

After this incident, the long peace between the Apaches and the white men came to an end. When General Carleton brought his California Column into New Mexico, the Chiricahuas prepared an ambush for the first units that entered Apache Pass. At a spring beside the now abandoned stagecoach station, the soldiers halted to fill their canteens, with infantry and cavalry strung out along the pass. Above them, five hundred warriors concealed in the rocky heights attacked with guns and arrows. In confusion the Californians hastily retreated. The Chiricahuas waited patiently for the soldiers to return for water at the spring. But

Indian tribes were drawn into the war in the Southwest when General Carleton's California Column marched into New Mexico to force Apaches and Navajos into reservation confinement.

when they did return they brought small cannons hidden in canvas-covered wagons. This time, superior firepower prevailed and the Apaches withdrew.

To General Carleton, an Apache was an Apache, and when he found it impossible to find and punish the elusive Chiricahuas he sent Lieutenant-Colonel Kit Carson after the accessible Mescaleros. Carson disliked the savagery of Carleton's orders—to kill on sight all adult males of the tribe and to take the women and children to Fort Stanton. Carleton's dictatorial power was the result of the martial law edict believed necessary by the federal government because of the Civil War threat from Texas.

Without informing Carleton, Kit Carson let it be known among the Mescaleros that any male Apache coming into Fort Stanton would be given protection from the squads of soldiers sent out along the Pecos to hunt them down.

General Carleton, meanwhile, established a new post, Fort Sumner, near a stand of cottonwoods on the Pecos that was known as the Bosque Redondo. There, the general decreed, the Mescaleros must live. The army would feed them if they followed Carleton's orders. They would be guarded by soldiers stationed at Fort Sumner, and any who escaped would be hunted down and killed.

Next the general turned his attention to the Navajos. As early as 1851, the army had built Fort Defiance at the mouth of the Borita Canyon in the Navajo country. Little trouble occurred between the soldiers and the Navajos until tension between the opponents in the white man's Civil War spread into the West. The fort had been built on grazing land long used by the Navajos. Their horses and sheep grazed there without hindrance until the fort's commander decided the increasing number of soldiers stationed there needed all the grass for their mounts. He ordered the Navajos to keep their livestock off the pastureland. The Navajos, however, had no fences, and one day when their animals gathered to graze, the soldiers marched out of the fort and slew them all.

Subsequent and similar events led two leaders of the Navajos, Manuelito and Barboncito, to assemble more than a thousand fighters. They surrounded Fort Defiance and attacked on three sides. They came close to victory, but eventually the soldiers' weapons overcame the Navajos' arrows and old Spanish guns.

This was the situation when General Carleton came to take command at Santa Fe. As soon as the Mescaleros were imprisoned, the general informed the Navajo leaders that if they wished to avoid war they should prepare their people for removal to the Bosque Redondo to join the Mescaleros. In the early summer of 1863, Carleton set a July deadline for removal. This order was a severe blow to a basically peaceable, agricultural people who raised sheep and goats and cultivated wheat, corn, beans, and fruit. After a few days of consultation, the Navajos decided to defend themselves in their Canyon de Chelly stronghold.

In July, Carleton ordered Kit Carson to begin a scorched earth campaign throughout the Navajo homeland, destroying hogans, the Navajo's dwellings, killing livestock, and burning fields of wheat and beans. Because of the strong resistance of a small group of fighters, Colonel Carson was unable to capture many Navajos for transport to the Bosque Redondo. This led General Carleton to issue an order to kill Navajo males on sight.

A peaceable agricultural tribe, the Navajos were rounded up and driven from their homeland of sheep and goats, grain fields and fruit orchards, into a dismal reservation—the Bosque Redondo on the Pecos—to share living space with similarly confined Apaches. There they endured until the Civil War was ended.

In late autumn, small bands began to surrender in order to keep the women and children from starving and freezing. By early March 1864, three thousand had surrendered. During the early spring months the infamous "Long March" of the Navajos was set in motion. It was a three-hundred-mile ordeal on foot, and many died on the way. The Navajos were now dependent upon the military for food and clothing. They were prisoners in the Bosque Redondo, a location unsuited for the raising of crops or livestock.

Not until the end of the distant Civil War—which had largely been the cause of their terrible displacement—were the Navajos allowed to return to their homeland.

On the Minnesota frontier, the Civil War was also indirectly responsible for breaking the long peace between the settlers and the four tribes of the Santee, or woodland Sioux. For half a century before the war, government officials had been chipping away at the Santees' lands, squeezing the Indians into smaller and smaller tracts along the Minnesota River. The wild game was almost gone by the time of the Civil War, making the tribes more dependent on the government for the necessities of life. Unfortunately for the Indians, the federal agents were more corrupt than usual. The agents established a credit system for the Santees. The Santees could obtain food supplies from the agency warehouses, but when the annuity funds came from Washington the agents had first claim upon the money, often cheating the Indians with falsified accounts and exorbitant interest. In the summer of 1862, the Santees were told that because of the Civil War, the government had no money to pay annuities owed them for giving up their lands. Since that year was a poor one for crops, the tribes had almost no food and no funds to buy food from the agency.

In July, Little Crow and other leaders assembled at the Upper Agency on Yellow Medicine River and asked Thomas Galbreath, the agent, to issue provisions from the warehouse, which was filled with contracted supplies. Galbreath refused, saying the Santees must wait for the delayed annuity payments. Then he summoned a company of soldiers to guard the warehouse. A few days later several hundred Santees surrounded the guards while others broke into the warehouse and brought out flour and other provisions. No violence occurred, and Little Crow asked Galbreath to distribute similar amounts of food from the Lower Agency, downriver at Redwood.

At Redwood, however, traders controlled the supplies and they refused to distribute any food until the annuities arrived. Little Crow protested that they could not get the money promised them, and that his people were starving. At this point a trader named Andrew Myrick spoke the oft-quoted words that were the spark to set off the disaster that followed: "If they're hungry, let them eat grass or their own dung."

The biggest losers in the Civil War in the West were the native peoples. From the forests of Minnesota across the Great Plains to Sand Creek, and in the deserts of the Southwest, Indian tribes were directly or indirectly caught up in the conflict.

Three days later the fury of the Santees exploded with an attack upon the Lower Agency by a force led by Little Crow. Andrew Myrick was among the twenty defenders killed. The warriors stuffed his mouth with grass. A general war broke out across southern Minnesota. The Santees besieged Fort Ridgely for three days, but were unable to capture it. They attacked the town of New Ulm and burned many buildings. The defenders suffered about a hundred dead and wounded, but they finally drove the warriors away. At Birch Coulee the Santees were winning when the arrival of mounted soldiers forced them to leave the field. And then the tide turned at Wood Lake, where a reinforced army of state militiamen defeated the Indians. Many white captives were freed, and many Santees were killed or taken prisoner.

Since the captured Santees were considered to be insurgents, some were given military trials. Three hundred and three were condemned to death for participating in the uprising, and the court-martial papers were sent to President Lincoln for review. Busy as he was with the Civil War battles in the East, Lincoln took the time to differentiate between those who were outright murderers and those who had engaged only in battle. He informed the Minnesota authorities that only thirty-nine of the three hundred and three condemned Santees should be hanged. And so ended the 1862–63 war of the woodland Sioux in Minnesota.

No military action during the Civil War has been more severely condemned than the assault of the Colorado Volunteers against the Cheyennes at Sand Creek. Through the many years since the event, the two words "Sand Creek" have become anathema to all American Indians.

By 1864, the Southern Cheyennes, under the leadership of Black Kettle, were eager to live in peace on the Colorado plains. The tribal leaders visited the Colorado governor in Denver in hopes of a treaty arrangement, but the governor rejected their overtures. Black Kettle then attempted an agreement with the army commander at Fort Lyon to establish a Cheyenne village near the fort to be under protection of the fort's soldiers.

The woodland Sioux fled to Canada. Some survivors of Sand Creek sought havens with their Northern Cheyenne relatives. Others went to the Antelope Hills in Indian Territory where Custer attacked them in the snow.

Again the chief was rebuffed. He was told to take his people to Sand Creek.

In one of his previous meetings with government officials, Black Kettle was given a large American flag and was told that if he kept the flag flying over his tepee, soldiers would never attack him. The Sand Creek encampment, however, seems to have been a prearranged trap, involving the governor, the Fort Lyon commander, and Colonel John Chivington of the Colorado Volunteers.

During the early dawn of November 29, Chivington's mounted forces struck the peaceful Cheyenne camp without warning. The troops were given orders to take no prisoners. No heed was paid to Black Kettle's American flag and the white flag of peace, but he and his wife miraculously escaped by hiding in a ditch.

Carbine and mortar fire slaughtered more than two hundred Cheyennes, mostly women and children. (The young warriors were away hunting buffalo on the adjoining Kansas plain.)

In the full light of morning, the Coloradans, many of whom were drunk, went over the scene of the massacre, scalping and mutilating the dead. Ears, fingers, and sexual organs were removed and taken into Denver. No effort was made to conceal the atrocities. When descriptions of the massacre spread across the nation, the revulsion was so great that Congress ordered an investigation. But those found guilty of atrocities were punished with little more than oral condemnation.

During the late months of the Civil War and into the bloody months of postwar retaliation by Indians on the Plains, a unique group of soldiers was sent into the West. They were former Confederate prisoners of war who obtained their freedom by taking an oath of allegiance to the Union and agreeing to serve as soldiers on the frontier.

They were organized into six regiments. The 1st and 4th Regiments manned five forts along the Missouri River, engaged in numerous skirmishes with hostile Indians, and fought gallantly in one bloody battle. Other regiments reopened stagecoach routes, restored mail service to California, escorted supply trains, and guarded the lonely and dangerous stations of telegraphers. They served in the Powder River Expedition of 1865, and fought in the Platte Bridge engagement. They escorted survey parties for the first transcontinental railroad. Officially the six regiments were known as United States Volunteers, but the world came to know them as Galvanized Yankees.

With the ending of the Civil War, peace was in the air in the West and new treaties were signed to mark new boundaries for the tribes.

CHAPTER SIX

RAILROADS WEST

As soon as railroads began supplanting rivers and canals for the transport of goods and people, the need for a transcontinental railway became apparent. No other invention could so swiftly bind together the East and the West. Without railroads, the West would have been settled a century later.

From the early years, planners thought of the transcontinental railroad as the *Pacific* Railroad. In the public consciousness, however, the building of this immense undertaking has usually been viewed as an east to west accomplishment. Actually, the most energetic force for the road originated in California.

Early in the decade preceding the Civil War, the U.S. Congress ordered the army to survey four different routes to the Pacific. One ran across the northern tier of states—St. Paul to Puget Sound. Another followed the 38th parallel from the Missouri frontier to San Francisco. A third was the 35th parallel beginning at Fort Smith, Arkansas. The fourth was a far southern route across Texas to southern California. The Secretary of War at the time was Jefferson Davis, later to become President of the Confederate States. Politics between North and South entered the controversy over a choice of routes, and delayed action until the war itself was under way.

Californians were disappointed by the delays, and in October 1859 they held a railroad convention in San Francisco to discuss ways and means of building a railway to the East. The leader of this movement was a Connecticut Yankee, an engineer named Theodore Judah who had come to California five years earlier to build the Sacramento Valley Railroad. Judah proposed that the transcontinental railroad be built straight through the Sierras from Sacramento. There was no need, he said, for a roundabout route north or south to avoid the mountains. Although his friends called him "Crazy Judah" for believing a railroad could cross the Sierras, they sent him to Washington to lobby for a railway to California.

It was largely through Judah's efforts that the Pacific Railroad Act of 1862 was passed, establishing methods for financing construction. None of the army's survey routes was chosen. With battles blazing in the Southwest it seemed only natural to follow the familiar old Oregon-California Trail, roughly along the 42nd parallel. The law, signed by President Lincoln on the day of a Union army retreat, provided that the two companies, the Central Pacific and the Union Pacific, would build from opposite ends of the transcontinental, receiving title to alternate sections of land on each side of the railroad, as well as subsidies in the form of bonds for each mile of track laid. Much more capital would be needed, of course, and Theodore Judah spent considerable time persuading four prosperous merchants to risk their fortunes on the Central Pacific.

Leland Stanford owned a wholesale grocery business and was running for governor of California. Collis Huntington and Mark Hopkins had built a miners' supply store into the largest hardware enterprise on the Pacific Coast. Charlie Crocker owned a big dry goods store. They would become the Big Four. After the death of Judah from yellow fever, which he caught on a Panama crossing, the energies and foresight of the Big Four pushed the Central Pacific through the Sierras, and made the four men very wealthy indeed. On January 8, 1863, a rousing groundbreaking ceremony was held in Sacramento.

Even before the Civil War, plans were under way for a transcontinental railroad. As soon as the war ended, the pace of construction accelerated, and steam locomotives drove into the Old West, some bringing outlaws.

Although horse-drawn stagecoaches were doomed by metal and steam, they remained important transportation connectors until the end of the nineteenth century.

Meanwhile, in the East, where the Civil War seemed increasingly stalemated, no enthusiasm had yet appeared. Not until October 1863 was a meeting held in New York to organize the Union Pacific. The Act that created the railroad required that two million dollars in stock had to be sold before construction could begin, and no single person could subscribe to more than two hundred shares.

For some years, Dr. Thomas Clark Durant had been a close observer of the movement to build a transcontinental railroad. Although he was a medical graduate, Durant discovered early in life that big money could be made speculating in railroad stocks, especially if the stock owner controlled the construction contracts involved in railroad building. Therefore Durant moved out in front of Ted Judah in pushing the Pacific Railway Act through Congress. He saw this as an arrangement that would involve numerous stock and bond transactions and construction contracts.

Durant was interested in, but not particularly excited by, the idea of a transcontinental railroad. He was, however, excited by the enormous fortune that financial manipulators could gain from it. The late Ted Judah, on the other hand, had been absorbed by the railroad itself. He cared little for the fortunes that could be made from it.

To gain control of the Union Pacific, Durant bought up the stock in the names of his friends, paying only the legal ten percent down payment, as specified in the railway act he helped to draft for Congress. Although Durant controlled enough stock to declare himself president of the Union Pacific, he stayed out of the limelight by arranging for an aging general, John A. Dix, to hold that office and serve as Durant's front man.

One of Durant's associates was George Francis Train, an eccentric young man who had made a fortune in shipping and railroads. Like Judah, Train cared little for the financial aspects, but was enthusiastic over the romance of a transcontinental railroad. He could not understand why the Union Pacific was so slow in getting construction started. Almost a year after the Central Pacific held its groundbreaking ceremonies in Sacramento, Train persuaded Durant that it was time for the Union Pacific to do likewise.

Since Omaha, Nebraska, had been chosen as the starting point for the Union Pacific, Train traveled there and organized a grand celebration for December 3, 1863. Several hundred people, including the governor of Nebraska, the railroad's engineer, Peter Dey, and two companies of artillery, gathered to hear Train deliver an impassioned speech in which he declared that the Pacific railroad was the nation, and the

When construction of the Union Pacific tracks fell behind schedule in the race with the Central Pacific, the promoters asked the advice of William T. Sherman, the famous Civil War general. Sherman visited the West and quickly perceived the incompetence of the engineer in charge. He recommended that he be replaced by General Grenville Dodge, who had built railroads quickly during the war. Under Dodge's guidance, track laying soon took on the aspects of an efficient military operation.

nation was the Pacific railroad. He concluded by shouting: "This is the grandest enterprise under God."

Engineer Peter Dey then read messages from President Lincoln and Dr. Durant. After the crowd cheered mightily and the artillery companies fired salutes, George Francis Train was certain that the railroad construction would start in a few days.

Engineer Dey did manage to assemble a small gang of workmen, and as soon as the prairie mud dried in the late spring, he supervised the grading of a few miles straight from Omaha. Back in New York, however, Durant was having trouble amassing credit and securing iron because of the voracious appetite of the Civil War. In California, the Big Four were faced with the same problems.

Not until the war ended did the nation's attention and energies turn toward the transcontinental railroad. Late in 1865, only a few months after Appomattox, steamboats in large numbers were churning up the Missouri River. Some were loaded with young men, veterans of the war looking for work. Other boats carried iron rails, spikes, shovels, tools, and an occasional locomotive. They were heading for Omaha, a frontier village that would become the nation's center until the Pacific railroad was completed. After a series of shady financial maneuvers and the passage of the second Pacific Railway Act—which doubled the amount of land received per mile of construction—Dr. Durant was ready at last to start spending other people's money. But first he pressured honest Peter Dey into resigning, and replaced him with Silas Seymour, a popinjay who prepared for his work on the prairie by donning a high-topped hat and carrying an umbrella to protect himself from the sun. His appearance amused the Pawnees who were daily spectators.

The first Union Pacific rail was laid on July 10, 1865. By this time the Central Pacific was fifty miles out of Sacramento, preparing to confront the mighty Sierras. On the flat plain of Nebraska, however, Seymour's crew was building only one mile a week. Frustrated because he needed completed mileage to collect from the government, Dr. Durant persuaded General William T. Sherman to visit Omaha to spur on the workmen and offer advice.

After examining the situation, Sherman apparently suggested that Durant fire Seymour and replace him with General Grenville Dodge, as chief engineer, and the Casement brothers, Jack and Daniel, as track-laying contractors. Not only were these men veterans of wartime transport accomplishments, but they were also experts in their fields and were honest and industrious.

With General Dodge out ahead with his surveyors, like an advance guard, track laying took on the aspects of a military operation. The Casement brothers selected about a thousand sturdy workers: veterans from both armies of the recent war, a considerable number of fresh Irish emigrants, and some former black slaves. They organized a work train of a dozen cars, each designed for a special purpose—a car filled with tools, one outfitted as a blacksmith shop, another with rough dining tables and a kitchen, others with built-in bunks, and several flat cars loaded with rails, spikes, fishplates, bolts, and ties.

As the work train began moving westward at an average of a mile a day, the Casements offered each workman a pound of tobacco if the mile was reached before sundown. A mile and a half a day of track laid brought an extra dollar; two miles by sundown brought double pay.

On August 1, the work train was one hundred and fifty miles west of Omaha, and by October, two hundred and fifty miles. Late in November, at the confluence of the North and South Platte rivers, the Casements put their men into tents for winter quarters. They named the place North Platte, and within a few weeks a hundred buildings arose—saloons, gambling dens, dance halls, hotels. This was the first of the rip-roaring, end-of-track towns that would follow the progress of the rails westward. From North Platte, each time the Union Pacific

Just as they had been drawn to rich pickings on stagecoaches,
western outlaws now turned to baggage and passenger trains.

established a supply camp at the end of the track, a town would spring up. Because many of the knockdown buildings were transported on flat cars from the previous boomtown to the next one, these mushroom towns were called "Hell on Wheels."

In California, during the closing months of 1865 and into 1866, the Central Pacific was climbing into the high slopes of the Sierras. Recognizing the difference between the level Great Plains and the rugged mountains, the government partially solved the financial problems of the Big Four by tripling the sixteen thousand dollars per completed mile that was originally granted. While Stanford, Huntington, and Hopkins sold bonds and lobbied governments, the other member of the Big Four, Charlie Crocker, served as general superintendent of the railroad. James Strobridge, the construction boss, was as capable a track builder as the Casements, but he had great difficulty finding and keeping good laborers. Young men coming from the East were looking for fortunes in gold and were not content to work at wage jobs. Finally, in desperation, Strobridge asked Crocker to find a continuous supply of labor; otherwise the Central Pacific could make little progress.

Crocker searched through the cities and towns of California, but the only dependable supply of laborers that he could find were Chinese. When he informed Strobridge of the situation, the construction boss replied that the Chinese were not strong enough to work as track builders.

"Did they not build the Chinese wall?" Crocker retorted, and directed Strobridge to try fifty men for a week. A week later, Strobridge asked for fifty more Chinese workers. Within a few weeks Crocker was hiring every able-bodied Chinese he could find, and then he sent off to China for more.

The Chinese proved to be especially proficient at cutting through granite rock to make tunnels and moving tons of earth and stone in wheelbarrows to build embankments around the faces of the Sierras. Thanks to their perseverance the Central Pacific marked the New Year of 1867 by boasting that the railroad was 5,911 feet above sea level, "a higher altitude than is attained by any other railroad in America." (Sherman Summit, at 8,235 feet on the Union Pacific in Wyoming, later claimed that honor.)

By the spring of 1868 the Chinese workers were building roadbeds down the eastern slope of the Sierras and into the arid flatlands of Nevada. The Union Pacific was nearing Utah. Soon the progress of the railroads became a race for mileage payments and land rights. The graders of both companies, being far out in front, began grading parallel roadbeds, passing each other in northern Utah. At last President Grant inter-

vened. He brought representatives of both railroads together, and a decision was made to join the two tracks together at Promontory Point, Utah.

The grand affair took place May 10, 1869. After a rainy night the weather cleared into an ideal day for celebration. All rails had been laid except for a two-rail gap where a huge American flag flapped atop an adjoining telegraph pole. Shortly after ten o'clock two Union Pacific trains arrived, the first one stopping a few yards from the gap in the rails. The first train was Durant's, carrying him and Grenville Dodge, the Casement brothers, and other officials and guests. Aboard the second train were four companies of infantry and their headquarters band, bound for the presidio in San Francisco.

At this time a group of Chinese workman appeared and began closing up the unfinished roadbed. They laid the last ties and rails, bolted on the fishplates, and drove all but the last few spikes, leaving space for one more tie. At 11:15 the Central Pacific train rolled into place. Both locomotives—the C.P.'s "Jupiter" with a funnel stack, and the U.P.'s No. 119 with cylindrical stack—were uncoupled and brought into facing positions.

By this time Leland Stanford and his group of officials were shaking hands with Dr. Durant and the Union Pacific representatives. None of those present who recorded the ceremony agreed on the number of people who gathered at that remote place in the West, but judging from the photographs the total was probably between six and seven hundred. Yet virtually all of America was aware of the importance of the day, and was there in spirit.

To speed the news of the joining of the rails, a wire was run down from the telegraph pole to a key on a small table facing the drivers of the last spikes. At 12:20 a laurel tie in which spike holes had previously been drilled was placed in position. The Reverend John Todd came forward and offered a short prayer. At 12:40 the telegrapher tapped out: "We have got done praying. The spike is about to be presented." Actually there were three or four spikes, of gold and silver. The point of a gold spike was placed in one of the narrow holes. Stanford raised his sledge, brought it down, and missed. Durant then raised his sledge, brought it down and missed. While the crowd of watching tracklayers roared with laughter, the telegrapher tapped out four letters: "DONE."

In cities across America, celebrations began while the small crowd at Promontory Point cheered, danced, and drank champagne. In Chicago the parade was seven miles long; in New York a hundred cannons fired salutes and Wall Street closed for the day; in Philadelphia bells were set to pealing all across the city; in Sacramento thirty gaily bedecked locomotives whistled in joyous concert; in San Francisco the celebration became a bedlam that lasted through the night.

But this was only the beginning. Four more transcontinental railroads were either under way or being planned in the fertile minds of restless engineers. Eventually, these railroads would tame the land, unite the nation, and bring an end to the Old West.

On May 10, 1869, the rails of the westbound Union Pacific and the eastbound Central Pacific were joined at Promontory Point, Utah. With the driving of a ceremonial golden spike, America's first transcontinental railroad came into being.

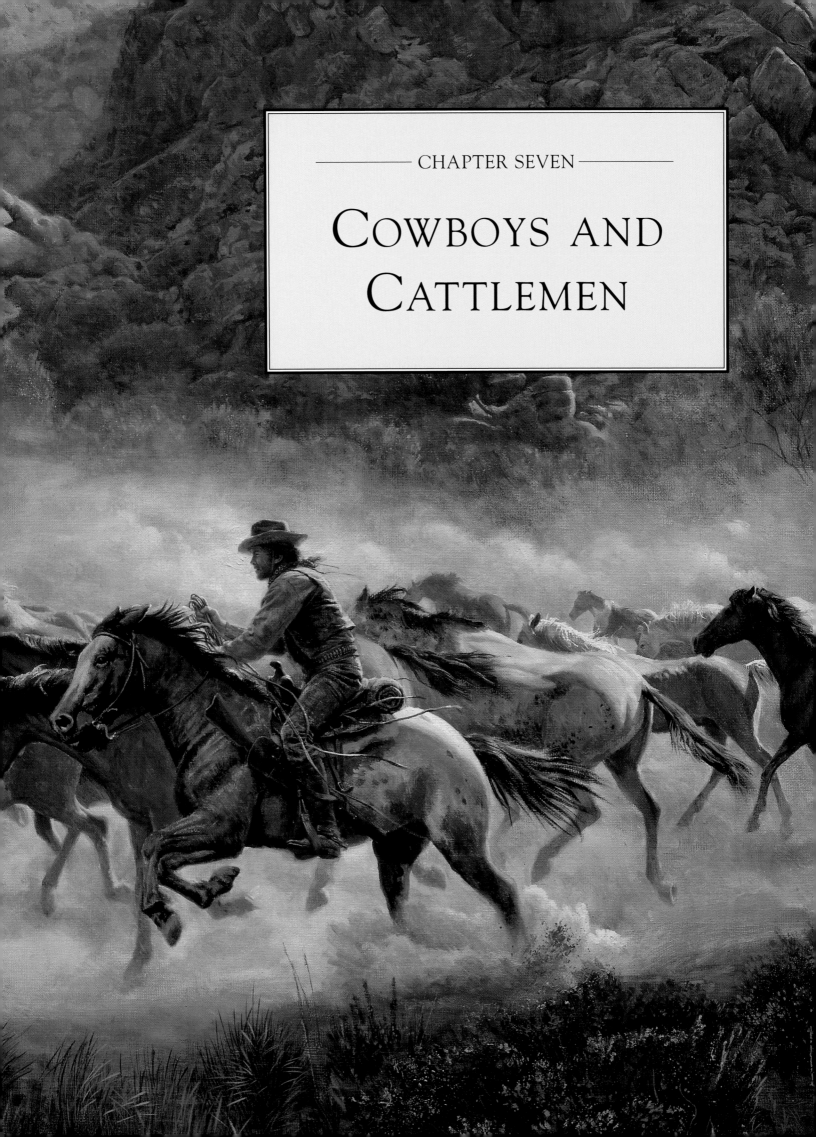

CHAPTER SEVEN

COWBOYS AND CATTLEMEN

Three centuries after Gregario de Villalobos, the young Spanish cattleman, brought his six heifers and a bull into Mexico at Vera Cruz, that Andalusian breed had spread by the thousands into the American Southwest. The cattle adapted and evolved on the grassy ranges, growing heavier, their horns lengthening. When Americans from the East began venturing into Texas they called these cattle Longhorns. By the time Texas won its independence, there were six Longhorns for each Texan, but because the big markets for beef were far away to the north and east, the cattle continued to multiply.

With the outbreak of the Civil War, a demand for beef came from the Confederate armies, and a few enterprising stockmen gathered herds together and drove them overland to Shreveport and New Orleans. But the larger military markets were too far to the east, and many of the young Texans were leaving the ranches to join in the fighting. At war's end, when the veterans began returning home, it seemed that all of Texas was filled with herds of cattle and horses roaming over the grasslands, the sparse brush country, and the dry plains.

At this same time, in the northern states there was a shortage of beef. On Christmas Day, 1865, on a 345-acre tract where several railroads converged, the Chicago Union Stock Yards opened for business, eager to obtain livestock to be converted to meat. By early spring of 1866 rumors were spreading through the Texas cattle country that in Chicago a five-dollar steer would bring forty dollars.

Like a spontaneous seasonal migration, cattle herds began moving north from Texas. The goals were the nearest railroads, and they were in Missouri; Sedalia was the choice railhead for Texans. After crossing Red River, the herds were driven on to Fort Gibson. In Indian Territory, some of the tribes demanded a ten-cent toll per head for crossing their allotted lands. Enduring fierce thunderstorms, unseasonably cold spring weather, flooded river crossings, and occasional stampedes, the cowboys and Longhorns reached the area of Baxter Springs, Kansas. Here the Texans encountered real trouble. Between Baxter Springs northeastward to the Sedalia railhead, the country was thickly settled by farmers. They did not want their fences wrecked and their crops trampled by herds of cattle.

Through that summer more than a thousand cattle were crowded onto pasturelands around Baxter Springs. The grass died or was burned off by angry farmers. Dishonest cattle buyers bought herds with bad checks. The unsold cattle began to die. By summer's end the great spontaneous drive of 1866 was ended. For the Texans it had been an inglorious bust.

After three centuries of adaptation, by the end of the Civil War Longhorn cattle filled the grasslands and plains of Texas. To get these cattle to markets in the North, Texas ranchers had to drive them overland to railroads in Missouri or Kansas.

As often happens when the world's affairs fall out of joint, one human being appears from somewhere to set in motion events that bring order out of chaos. In this instance it was Joseph McCoy of Springfield, Illinois, who saw the dilemma through the eyes of a stockman friend who had been caught in the Baxter Springs debacle. McCoy's solution was to build a cattle-shipping town on a railroad far west of settled farm country. He chose the Kansas Pacific, still under construction, at a settlement of log huts called Abilene. Nearby there was a river filled with water for thirsty Longhorns, and on the prairie for miles around was a sweeping sea of grass for restoring livestock at the end of an overland drive. McCoy built shipping pens and a hotel, and then sent messengers south into Texas, inviting cattlemen to drive their herds to an ideal place for selling and shipping cattle. Although the season was growing late before word could spread everywhere, cattle came to Abilene by the thousands. Thanks to Joseph McCoy the pattern was now set for the next quarter of a century for trail drives, cow towns, and the development of the great cattle industry of the Old West.

Now it was up to the ranchers to develop a more efficient system of roundups, branding, and drives to the market. By borrowing ideas from Mexico and adding practices that suited the varied Texas geography and herbage, the ranchers soon adapted an efficient routine for marketing their Longhorns.

The first order of business for a trail drive north was to bring the cattle in from the range to the main camp corral.

To begin a roundup, the cowboys canvassed the range in all directions, searching thickets and arroyos. In the early years the Longhorns were wild and had to be pulled out of the brush and chaparral by force, or lured out with tame cattle decoys. When tame cattle were mixed with wild Longhorns it was not too difficult to drive the herd to the main camp corral. The next step was to separate the mature animals, which were to be driven overland to market, and the calves, which were to be branded and returned to the range. "Cutting out," it was fittingly called, and required a well-trained pony, one that could "turn on a dime," and a rider who had a sharp eye and good muscular reflexes and who was an expert at handling a lariat. As soon as an unbranded animal was roped, it was quickly herded to the nearest fire, where branding irons were heated to an orange red. In Texas a law was passed requiring all cattle to be branded in a corral; its intention was to prevent rustlers from hastily branding stock on the open range.

Branding is as old as history, but the first recorded brand in North America was that of the conquistador Hernando Cortes, who seared three Christian crosses on the flanks of his livestock. The first brands in Texas were usually the initials of the owner and were registered in brand books. If two cattlemen had the same initials, a bar or a circle distinguished one from the other. Friction over the ownership of unbranded cattle, or suspicion of altered brands, caused occasional gunfights. Since many letters were easily changed, like C to an O, and F to an E, as time passed ranchers learned to design unusual brands, with such names and shapes as Stirrup, Dinner Bell, Frying Pan, Ox Yoke. After winning a large poker hand, one rancher designed his brand after the lucky cards, four sixes, said to be one of the more difficult brands to alter.

Roundups and trail drives required a plenitude of horses. Each man on a drive usually needed six mounts. From herds of wild horses they were rounded up much like cattle, and broken to the use of saddles.

Bad weather was one of the main hazards of a trail drive. An unexpected late-spring snowstorm was certain to slow the herd's movement to a railhead and bring misery to the cowboys. On the trail, right, the chuckwagon was hearth and home for the cowboys, with the cook serving as host and morale-builder.

As soon as the work of branding was completed at the roundup corral, the rancher, or his range boss, would complete preparations for a trail drive to market. The main requirement was a plenitude of horses. Wild horse herds were the original source, and they were rounded up much like wild cattle. After experiencing a few drives, cattlemen learned that each cowboy would need at least six horses—perhaps a mustang for "cutting out," a gentle mount for night herding—all of them sound enough to stay in good condition on a diet short on grain and long on prairie grass.

For the journey north to market with a herd of twelve hundred to two thousand cattle, a rancher would choose twelve to eighteen of his best cowboys, plus a cook and himself (or his foreman). Each man was allowed two blankets and a bag containing a change of clothing; these were hauled on the single supply wagon that might accompany the drive, or in the chuckwagon. Everything else the cowboy carried was on his person. He seldom wore a coat, because it restricted his movement, and if he wore a vest he seldom buttoned it, for he believed that to do so would cause him to get a bad cold. He wore chaps not to be picturesque but to protect his legs from underbrush and weather.

A cowboy would pay good money for a big hat because it was his roof against the elements; he wanted the brim wide to keep off rain, sun, and snow. A large bandanna was a prized possession, so essential that J. Frank Dobie cataloged dozens of uses—from dust mask to towel, blindfold for skittish horses, bandage, sling for a broken arm, face covering for dead cowboys, and on and on.

Cowboys on a trail drive dreaded thunderstorms and river
crossings. A bolt of lightning and a crack of thunder could start
a nervous cattle herd in a mad dash across the plain.

The Spanish-Mexican influence upon ranching in the Old West is shown in the nomenclature. *Chaparajos* became chaps, *la reata* changed to lariat, *cinca* to cinch, *cuarto* to quirt, *mesteño* to mustang, *lazo* to lasso. *Vaquero*, the cow herder, slowly evolved into cowboy. Kansas cow town newspapers of the early 1870s referred to trail drivers as drovers, herders, or simply "boys." Charles Goodnight of the famous JA Ranch usually called them "boys," but in recalling those days he noted: "We employed a little army of men called 'cowboys.'"

Getting a herd of two or three thousand cattle moving on the trail toward a shipping town was as complicated as starting an army on the march. To keep a herd in order, the trail boss usually searched out a huge domineering animal and put it in the lead position. After a day or so on the trail the cattle would fall into place behind the leader every morning, each one keeping the same relative position in the herd. In the order of movement, the trail boss rode two or three miles in advance. Behind him were the supply wagon and the chuckwagon, which was usually driven by the cook. On the left or right was the *remuda*, the herd of spare horses. Then came the point riders, one on each side of the lead cattle, keeping them on the trail. Along both sides of the widening flow of the herd were the swing and flank riders, their numbers determined by the size of the herd. Bringing up the rear were the drag riders, the least desirable assignment on a drive. All day they rode in clouds of dust and had to keep prodding the lagging cattle to maintain the pace of the herd.

On a long trail drive the chuckwagon became both hearth and home. The cook was expected to serve adequate fare and also act as a blacksmith, barber, surgeon, and morale builder. As for the vehicle, it was a work of utilitarian art, the invention of Charles Goodnight, the pioneer cattleman. The sturdy wagon was covered with canvas and equipped with a box at the rear for storing dishes and a Dutch oven, frying pan, kettle, and coffeepot. The standard staples also had their exact places—flour, coffee, an abundance of beans, cornmeal, and salt pork. If a supply wagon was not brought on the drive, the front of the chuckwagon was used to carry bedrolls, blankets, and extra clothing.

A trail herd traveled about fifteen miles a day, so that the drive might last for two or three months, depending on the distance from ranch to shipping town. The main hazards along the way were river crossings, lightning storms, and stampedes. A sudden bolt of lightning and a thunderclap could start a nervous herd moving in a frantic mass. The only way to stop the onrush was to ride toward the head of the stampede and turn the leaders by firing revolvers and forcing the cattle into a great milling circle.

The only way cowboys could stop frenzied animals was to turn the leaders of the herd in a milling circle—an exceedingly dangerous maneuver.

But at last, after enduring weeks of dust, mud storms, short rations, and stampedes, most of the cattle, horses, and men survived to hear the whistle of a railroad train. At first sight of the sprawling false fronts of a cow town's plank buildings, the cowboys would lift their hats and break into wild yells.

To reach a railroad shipping town from the east Texas grasslands or the dry plains of west Texas required well-planned trails. Water and grass along the way were essential. The legendary Chisholm Trail derived from a trading route marked out by Jesse Chisholm, the Scots-Cherokee frontiersman. Chisholm traded with tribes in Indian Territory and needed a road to connect his trading posts between Kansas and Red River.

After Joseph McCoy developed Abilene's shipping facilities, he extended the trail to Fort Worth. Within three or four years, the Chisholm became the main artery for several other connecting trails—the Eastern, which brought King Ranch and other cattle from the Gulf of Mexico coastlands, and the Western, originating in San Antonio, parts of which became known as the Dodge City Trail. As railroads and settlements moved westward in the 1870s, the shipping towns also moved westward, and old trails were altered and new trails created. Charles Goodnight and his partner, Oliver Loving, pioneered a trail westward into New Mexico to sell beef to military contractors, and it was named for them. After Loving's death, Goodnight drove cattle north into Colorado and Wyoming, and his route became the Goodnight Trail. Since that trail extended into Montana, with branches from western Kansas, the cattlemen fittingly dubbed this last great overland cattle road the Texas Trail.

The men who pioneered the cattle drives, who chose the trail routes, who built great ranches, and who improved the breeds, were extraordinary human beings. As Frederick Remington said, they were men with the bark on. Richard King was among the earliest. In 1835, at the age of eleven, he stowed away on a ship that was docked in New York City and bound for Mobile. He was discovered by the captain and put to work. At Mobile the captain helped him find work on a river steamer. By 1846 he was operating his own steamboat on the Rio Grande. In 1852, riding with a young army captain named Robert E. Lee (on duty in Brownsville), he followed a trail across the flats between the Nueces and the Rio Grande. King remarked on the luxuriant grass along the coastland, saying he thought it would be fine for cattle raising if there was only a market for beef. Lee replied that possibly a market could be found if a man tried hard enough.

The next year King bought a Spanish land grant that contained the grasslands, seventy-five thousand

Cattle approaching a river crossing were usually thirsty and tended to bunch up along the banks.
Cowboys risked their lives and sometimes lost them while driving a herd into and across a river.

acres. With his steamboat earnings he acquired Longhorns and horses and employed a small army of Mexican *vaqueros*. In the year before the Civil War he formed a partnership with an old steamboating friend, Mifflin Kennedy. They increased their land holdings and imported Durhams from Kentucky to improve the stock.

With the coming of the Civil War, the steamboats were in demand for hauling cotton downriver to the gulf to load onto British merchant ships. Unlike many Texans during the war, King and Mifflin prospered. In the years immediately following the war, the cattle trails to Kansas offered even more riches for the King Ranch's Running W brand.

Another famed rancher of the Old West was Abel "Shanghai" Pierce. Like Richard King he was a stowaway. At a Virginia port he boarded a ship that was bound for Indianola, Texas. Pierce had no desire to be a sailor. He was twenty years old and had no trouble finding work on a ranch. Six years later he owned his own spread on the grassy coastland of Matagorda Bay. Then the Civil War interrupted, and Pierce joined the Confederate army. When the war ended he returned to his ranch and was one of the first Texas cattlemen to drive Longhorns to Kansas.

Pierce was tall, muscular, and full-bearded; his jovial manner and booming voice attracted friends and created legends. Supposedly his nickname "Shanghai" originated from a remark he made about a pair of oversized spurs a salesman had foisted off on him: "These things make me look like an old Shanghai rooster!" In his later years he paid a large sum for a twenty-foot bronze statue of himself and had it set up on his ranch. Today it stands guard over his grave.

After the trails from the cattle country lengthened to Wyoming and Montana, the cowboys learned to prepare for snow, early and late.

Pierce's greatest contribution to the cattle industry was his importation of Brahman cattle, which were immune to tick fever, then prevalent. These were the foundation stock for the American Brahmans now bred across the country. Following Pierce's lead, the King ranch crossed Brahmans with Shorthorns to create the famous Santa Gertrudis cattle.

With the passage of time, however, it is Charles Goodnight who stands out as the giant among all the pioneer cattlemen of the Old West. Goodnight was born in the Middle West and never had any experience with ships or the sea, but like King, at the age of eleven he left his home for Texas. That was in 1846, when his stepfather and mother put him on an unsaddled horse in Macoupin County, Illinois, to ride with them to the Texas frontier. Ten years later Goodnight and his stepbrother were rounding up and branding Longhorns near Fort Belknap for overland drives to New Orleans. The pay and profits were meager, and when the Civil War began he joined a Confederate company of mounted riflemen to patrol the Red River border of Texas and Indian Territory.

At the war's end, instead of joining the mobs of ranchers driving Longhorns to Missouri Trailheads, Goodnight and his neighbor Oliver Loving drove a herd to New Mexico and received good prices for their beef from government contractors at Fort Sumner. The imprisoned Navajos and Mescaleros were still there and in need of rations.

During the next few years, Goodnight continued driving his cattle to New Mexico, and extended his trail to the Colorado mining towns. But when he attempted ranching near Pueblo, and started his own bank there, he ran headlong into the Panic of 1873 and came near to losing everything. He and his wife assembled a small group of cowboys and drove what was left of the herd back to Texas. This time Goodnight chose the Palo Duro Canyon in the Panhandle for his ranch. To obtain finances for the purchase of Durham bulls to upgrade his Longhorn stock, he formed a partnership with John G. Adair, a wealthy Briton.

This was the beginning of the famous JA Ranch. Eleven years later, when the partnership ended, the Palo Duro was filled with one hundred thousand cattle. During those years, most of the Longhorns were replaced with Herefords.

After leaving the JA, Goodnight started his own ranch again. He was now wealthy enough to have a town named for him on the nearby railroad. As he grew older, he became more eccentric, treating his cowboys like children, forbidding them to play cards, to use profanity, to drink whiskey. Yet there were always men eager to work for him.

On a diet of beef and black coffee, and sometimes a full box of Cuban cigars a day, Charles Goodnight lived until 1929, when he died at the age of ninety-three, the last of the pioneer cattlemen of the Old West.

With the introduction of fences and the closing of the open range, ranching became more competitive —more prosperous for some, less prosperous for others. Disputes over such issues as land claims, water rights, illegal branding, and rustling sometimes resulted in range wars like the Lincoln County War in New Mexico and the Johnson County War in Wyoming. Violated boundary lines almost surely caused gunplay.

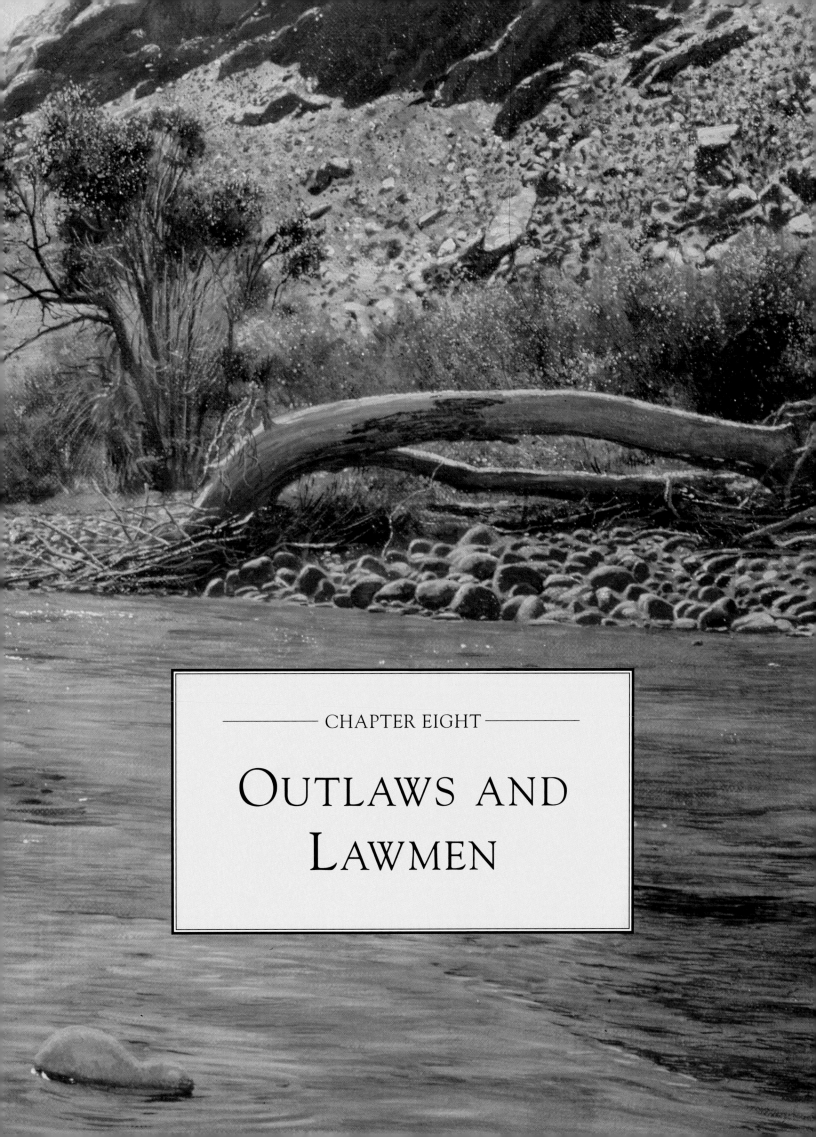

CHAPTER EIGHT

OUTLAWS AND LAWMEN

The Homestead Act that Congress passed during the Civil War, plus the availability of land from the transcontinental railroads, brought millions of immigrants into the West during the 1870s. As more railroads pushed westward, more towns were formed to boom and bust, or to boom and prosper.

Cattle-shipping towns and mining towns all boomed because of the rapid rises in population. Most of the first inhabitants of these settlements were men— cowboys or miners, gamblers, saloon keepers. Quick money and an anarchic environment often led to lawlessness and violence. Many of the Texans who were bringing cattle into Kansas were Confederate veterans. Many of the men they confronted in shipping towns were Union veterans, or soldiers from nearby forts. The war was only a decade past, and partisan feelings sometimes ran high.

To keep order in the cow towns, the business leaders usually employed lawmen who had considerable experience with firearms and violence. In many of these men, the line between lawman and outlaw was rather thin. Luke Short, for example, started out as a cowboy, broke the law by selling whiskey to Indians, killed men through trickery, but sometimes worked as a lawman. And "Rowdy Joe" Lowe tried being a lawman, but found lawlessness more profitable. "Mysterious" Dave Mather, another example, moved back and forth from confidence games and train robberies to serving as constable and marshal. Early in their careers, Wild Bill Hickok and Wyatt Earp were sometimes on the shady side of the law. The Thompson brothers, Ben and Billy, were incorrigible youths from Yorkshire, England, who emigrated to Texas in 1849. Ben's first victim was another teenager whom he shot in the back. Before embarking on a career as a marshal of Austin, Texas, he spent considerable time flouting the law. He was in Abilene, Kansas, the first year of Joseph McCoy's cattle-shipping pens.

Ben Thompson and his crony Phil Coe opened the Bull's Head gambling saloon in Abilene about the time the authorities of that boisterous town hired Wild Bill Hickok to keep the peace. Hickok had gained his reputation as the tamer of Hays City, a wild railroad town. One of Hickok's first assignments in Abilene was to order Thompson and Coe either to remove or to alter a huge advertisement on the wall of the Bull's Head. It was a wall-sized painting of a very lascivious bull, and several citizens had protested its shamelessness.

When Hickok confronted Thompson, the saloon keeper refused to take any action about the bull. Whereupon the marshal bought a bucket of paint and "materially altered the offending bovine." Neither Thompson nor Coe took any counteraction at the time, but later events indicated that both resolved to even the score with Wild Bill in the future.

One of the cowboys who came to Abilene that season was an eighteen-year-old named John Wesley Hardin. He had already achieved considerable notoriety with his reckless use of firearms. When Ben Thompson met him he tried to prejudice the boy against Wild Bill.

"Marshal Hickok is a Yankee," Thompson told Hardin. "He picks out southern men to kill, especially Texans."

During the decade following the Civil War, millions of immigrants poured into the West. The Homestead Act and inexpensive land, which was available from the transcontinental railroads, facilitated the acquisition of farms and ranches. During the early years of settlement on the treeless Great Plains, sodhouses were the cheapest and quickest means of sheltering a family. Three-foot blocks of thick sod plowed from half an acre of prairie would build a one-room house. Except for leaking and occasionally falling roofs, the sodhouses were comfortable and had a lifespan of about seven years.

"If Wild Bill needs killing," Hardin replied, "why don't you kill him yourself?"

Hardin next called on Hickok to gauge his mettle. The marshal showed him a handbill he had received from Texas offering a reward for the capture of Hardin, wanted for murder. Hickok told him he would not arrest him for crimes committed in Texas, but that if he shot anyone in Abilene he would not get out of town alive. Hardin's career as an outlaw was only beginning, but he and Hickok had no further meetings.

Before the end of that booming season of 1871, however, Wild Bill and Phil Coe of the Bull's Head saloon met in an Old West showdown. Apparently, the growing enmity of the two had been enhanced by their rivalry for the favors of a dance-hall girl named Jessie Hazel. One evening while Hickok was gambling in the Novelty Bar, he heard a gunshot across the street in front of the Alamo. When he went to investigate he found Phil Coe holding a gun in his hand. There were several variations of what happened next, but the affair ended with Hickok deliberately shooting Coe to death and also, accidentally, killing his own deputy.

After that, Hickok was finished in Abilene, and the town's leaders decided they had endured enough violence from gamblers and cowboys. Certain that the gamblers would leave if no cowboys came to Abilene, the city council passed an ordinance in February 1872 banning any further shipments of Texas cattle from the town. Copies were printed and sent to Texas. Abilene wanted no more cowboys, and to prove it they held an agricultural fair for the farmers and the new settlers in the county. A year later the shipping business was so bad that Abilene was begging the cattlemen and shippers to come back, but it was too late. To the west, new boomtowns were already in the making.

The town of Newton was the choice for the next season, largely because Joseph McCoy came there from Abilene to build shipping pens. Newton was on the Atchison, Topeka & Santa Fe Railroad, a rival of the Kansas Pacific across Kansas, although their final destinations of Santa Fe and Denver were far apart. During the next decade the preferred cow towns would alternate from railroad to railroad, ever moving westward. And the outlaws and lawmen would follow the boomtowns.

Gunfire was frequent enough in Newton to warrant the hiring of a Santa Fe railroad workman to keep the peace. He was a burly Irishman named Mike McCluskie. In the course of his duties he killed a Texas gambler. A few evenings later, while McCluskie was playing faro in Perry Tuttle's dance hall, High Anderson, a gunfighter and a friend of the dead gam-

The legendary dissension between the gunfighter and the lawman is a continuation of people's ancient conflict with good and evil. After seeing the depiction in numerous movies, television dramas, and Western novels, the whole world knows the ritual of the outlaw and the lawman facing each other in a dusty street, their hands ready to draw their Colt .45s. More often than not the lawman had been a gunfighter, and frequently the embittered outlaw was a former lawman. The line between the two was often finespun.

bler, suddenly confronted McCluskie. In the next moments one of the deadliest gunfights in the history of the Old West exploded into action. Anderson put three bullets into McCluskie before the lawman could respond. A noisy gun battle quickly broke out between McCluskie's railroad friends and Anderson's cowboy friends. At the end of the firing, five men were dead, five were wounded. It was a bloodier affair than the celebrated O.K. Corral confrontation, which resulted in casualties of three, or the gun battle in Wyatt Earp's Tombstone, Arizona, during which three were killed. Newspapers dubbed it the Newton General Massacre, but it failed to become a legend like the Earp-Clanton feud. After all, the principals were all dead before they became famous, leaving no Doc Hollidays or Wyatt Earps to create a mythology of gunfighters in Newton.

Now it was Ellsworth's turn, on the Kansas Pacific. The railroad and the cattle traders joined to survey a new trail southeast to the old Chisholm route, naming it the Ellsworth Trail. A guide map was published and distributed across Texas, advertising a new trail from Red River Crossing "to the Old Reliable Kansas Pacific Railway."

By the end of May 1873, one hundred thousand cattle were grazing around Ellsworth, and when another fifty thousand arrived in June, the market collapsed. This temporary setback did not deter the usual challengers of the law. Ben Thompson and his brother, Bully Bill, arrived to set up a gambling concession in the Grand Central Hotel. It was predictable that one of the brothers would be involved in gunplay before the season ended. During a drunken brawl, Billy shot and killed Ellsworth's popular lawman, Chauncey Whitney, who had lived there since the town's beginnings. A survivor of the Beecher Island fight, Whitney apparently had no fear of ruffians. Billy Thompson shot him in a drunken rage, and brother Ben had to spirit him out of town to avoid a lynching.

In spite of all the efforts of the Kansas Pacific Railroad to keep Ellsworth the preeminent cow town, the Santa Fe took the lead again when it pushed southwestward to Wichita. As a cattle-shipping point, Wichita was far enough south of Ellsworth to cut about a week off a trail drive from Texas. Beginning with its first weeks, Wichita's promoters were determined not to fall too early into the trap of respectability and law enforcement that might drive away cowboys and other visitors. A few miles down the Ellsworth Trail signs were posted: EVERYTHING GOES IN WICHITA.

This easygoing attitude attracted lawless characters as well as cattlemen and their cowboys. Ben

Neither outlaws nor lawmen believed it possible to survive on the frontier without a horse and a handgun or a shoulder weapon, preferably both. Some pistoleers required two guns in opposite holsters, loose and ready for quick double draws. Without horses, lawmen could not pursue outlaws fleeing from the towns, nor could outlaws escape from the towns. Except for a few gunmen, like the Daltons and the Earp brothers and their associates, tracking outlaws or escaping from the law on horseback was something a man did alone. Unless he needed help to stop and rob a train, even the convivial Jesse James often chose to ride alone.

Thompson was an early arrival, setting up his gambling tables in the Keno House. A casual visitor was a young man in his mid-twenties named Wyatt Earp. He had worked as a buffalo hunter and a stagecoach driver, and he did a bit of prizefighting and gambling. He spent some time in Ellsworth and was offered a job as a lawman there, but he turned it down. Shortly after arriving in Wichita to visit his brother, James, who was a bartender, he was invited to become a deputy marshal and he accepted.

One of Earp's first encounters was with George Peshaur, a big blustering gunslinger. Ben Thompson had told Peshaur that Wyatt Earp hated Texans and needed to be driven out of Wichita. When Peshaur stopped Earp on the street one day and accused him profanely of being a coward, the deputy marshal, instead of drawing a gun, challenged Peshaur to a fistfight. Earp blackened both of his eyes and smashed his nose.

In a move to even the score, Peshaur persuaded his friend Mannen Clements to assemble a gang of cowboys from the Clement's cow camp to hurrah the town of Wichita and its lawmen, especially Wyatt Earp.

From a friend, Earp received information that Clements and his gang would be coming into town across the toll bridge that led onto Douglas Avenue. Most likely, the friend said, they would come shortly after sunrise, a time most of the population would be asleep after the usual night of revelry.

Undertaking the task of stopping the raid, Earp assembled a small posse, placed the best marksmen in strategic positions along Douglas Avenue facing the bridge, and waited. When the raiders arrived, they halted at the opposite end of the bridge, dismounted, and with weapons at the ready, started to cross the bridge. Recognizing Clements, who was leading the mob, Earp called out: "Mannen, holster your guns and take your boys back to camp."

"You holster your guns," Clements replied, "and maybe I will."

Earp slid his guns into their holsters. Clements stared at him for a moment, then holstered his weapons and ordered his men to mount up and return to camp.

Why a lawless man like Clements, an accused cattle rustler, cruel feudist, and cousin of the notorious John Wesley Hardin, would obey Earp's command is one of the mysteries surrounding Wyatt Earp. The lawman's contemporaries believed there was something in Earp's demeanor that inspired obedience. Whatever it was, Earp became one of the most enduring of the Old West's mythical law-and-order characters, his deeds continually recounted in our popular culture of Western novels, films, and television.

Meanwhile, the Kansas Pacific Railroad was trying to regain some of its lost revenue by transforming Hays City into a cow town. Hays owed its origins to Fort Hays, and was a wild place before Joseph McCoy created Abilene. Its dance halls, saloons, and gambling establishments provided a playground for a mixed crowd of buffalo hunters, railroad workers, and soldiers from the fort. Wild Bill Hickok served as sheriff of the county before he went east to Abilene.

To supply goods and services to the growing populations, towns flourished along railroads and rivers. Boomtowns usually attracted lawless elements, and the legendary lawmen of the Old West soon appeared upon the scene.

When Texans were persuaded to drive their trail herds to Hays City, it was inevitable that clashes would occur between former Confederates and Union cavalrymen from the fort. The life of Hays City as a cow town was boisterous, but brief. And Wichita on the Santa Fe Railroad was also about to lose its title to a town that in 1872 had consisted of a single shack where whiskey was sold to railroad workmen. Nearby was Fort Dodge and the Santa Fe Trail. As soon as railroad tracks were completed, hordes of buffalo hunters began bringing in hides for shipment. In 1873, they shipped two hundred thousand hides, and a town began building around the railroad station. A year later, cattle-loading pens were constructed and Dodge City was on its way to becoming "the cowboy capital," the wildest and longest lived of all cattle-shipping towns. Cattle were shipped not by the hundred thousands but by the millions.

For a golden decade money flowed, luring gamblers, prostitutes, outlaws, entertainers, lawyers, doctors, newspapermen, and the curious. Almost every name in the nation's pantheon of outlaws and lawmen came to Dodge City at least once.

Luke Short ran the gambling concession in the Long Branch saloon, employing the first female piano player to perform in a Dodge saloon. She drew so many cowboys away from the mayor's Alamo dance hall that he had an ordinance passed prohibiting female piano players in Dodge. As soon as Luke Short reluctantly let the pianist go, the mayor repealed the law and hired her for the Alamo.

Folklore tells us that during the town's first big season, twenty-four men were killed in gunfights, making it necessary to open a cemetery. Because all its inhabitants died with their boots on, it was named Boot Hill. Twenty-four may have died with their boots on, but not likely from gunfire. After searching records of town and country, Robert Dykstra, an authority on Western literature, found that during Dodge's ten wildest years a total of only fifteen died from gunfire.

Lawmen respected the marksmanship, endurance, and obstinacy of most of their adversaries, but would risk their lives to hunt down a rogue outlaw.

Among the keepers of the peace in Dodge were Wyatt Earp, Bat Masterson, Mysterious Dave Mather, Bill Tilghman, and Charlie Bassett. Masterson was probably the most popular of the lawmen, but Earp built his reputation for enforcement, fearlessness, and marksmanship during the time he was in Dodge. To keep the gunslingers out of such fancy night places as the Long Branch and Lady Gay, he established the Deadline, forbidding guns north of the railroad track.

Earp also organized one of the most dramatic manhunts (which has become the basis for much fiction and film) to avenge the fatal shooting of Dodge City's most beloved female entertainer. She was Dora Hand, who performed as Fannie Keenan, singing in the Comique Theater as well as in the better dance halls. According to rumor, she was from a fine old Boston family.

A wealthy Texan named James Kennedy fell in love with Dora while she was performing at James Kelley's Alhambra. But Dora had chosen another suitor, and rebuffed Kennedy. One evening when Kennedy annoyed her, Kelley threw him out of the Alhambra.

Not long afterward, late in the night, Kennedy rode up to Kelley's house and fired four shots into the bedrooms. Kelley was away, however, and one shot went into a bedroom occupied by Dora Hand and her roommate, an actress. Miss Hand was killed instantly.

By dawn the identity of the assailant was known. Wyatt Earp's blue-ribbon posse of veteran lawmen consisted of himself, Bat Masterson, Charlie Bassett, Bill Tilghman, and several lesser known gunfighters. Through the years, details of this pursuit have undoubtedly been embellished. Each lawman supposedly rode with a spare mount, so that they could use their horses alternately, while Kennedy had only one horse. The pursuit ended almost at the Texas border, forty or fifty miles from Dodge. When Kennedy's horse collapsed, he used the dying animal as a barricade against his pursuers and did not surrender until he was shot in the arm. The lawmen took him back to Dodge and kept a mob from lynching him until he could be tried by a jury. Kennedy, however, managed to convince judge and jury that his intention had been to kill James Kelley and not the love of his life, Dora Hand. Kennedy was declared not guilty and returned to Texas.

Such raw material for tales of the Old West grew scarcer in the cattle-shipping towns during the 1880s. Dodge City was the last, and like its predecessors was soon surrounded by farms and small ranches. Tick fever made Texas cattle unwelcome. Towns along the whole western frontier began to resemble towns in the East, with schools, churches, business houses, and permanent dwellings. Railroads extended their tracks into all parts of the cattle-raising country so that trail drives were no longer necessary.

The gamblers and outlaws were soon drifting off to the untamed mining towns farther west—to places like Tombstone, Deadwood, and Virginia City in Nevada, and Virginia City in Montana. With ill-gotten gains, many an outlaw went to San Francisco to spend his lucre on high living.

Lawmen made their reputations tracking killers, capturing them, and bringing them back to town for trial. Wyatt Earp once led a fifty-mile horseback pursuit of a killer, and brought him back to Dodge City. The image on the right tells the story—a cold and weary but disdainful lawman, ignoring the captive except for the lead rope, the defeated outlaw gripping his wounded arm. It is a chilly gray morning after a rain—so early that the streets are empty, the smithy and Wells Fargo are closed, and not one of the girls in Amy's Place is to be seen.

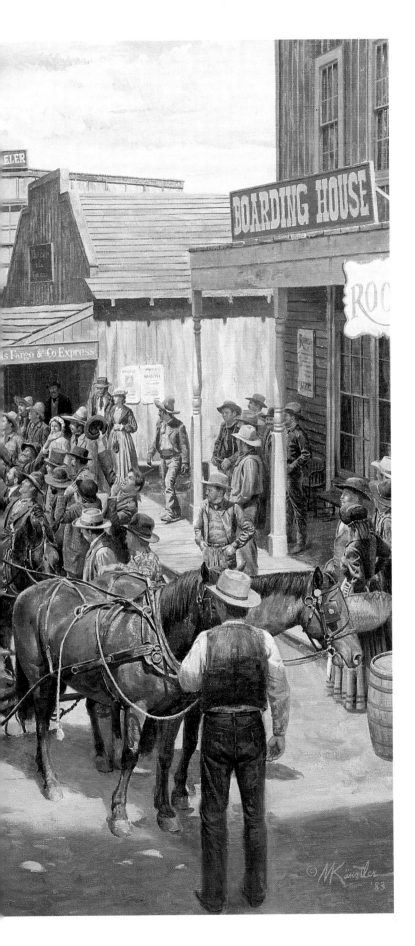

Marshals and sheriffs dressed very much like Mississippi riverboat gamblers, which some of them had been earlier in their careers. After keeping the peace for a time in a rough town like Dodge City, the lawmen often obtained financial interests in saloons and dance halls. The town marshal was usually among the most interested observers when a stagecoach stopped to unload some new girls. He might view them as welcome additions to the town or as competition for his dance-hall girls.

Before they left Dodge City for good, Wyatt Earp and his friend Doc Holliday visited Deadwood the year after Wild Bill Hickok had gone there in hopes of striking it rich. Instead of finding a gold mine, Hickok was shot, in the back, by a glory-seeking derelict named Jack McCall. Earp and Holliday did not strike it rich either, but returned to Dodge until the action there ran out.

In the 1880s, with Doc Holliday and his brothers Virgil and Morgan, Wyatt Earp more or less became the authority figure in Tombstone, Arizona, a town based upon rich silver mines. In 1881 a feud erupted between the Earps and the Clanton gang. The showdown came, as every fan of popular culture knows, at the O.K. Corral. The names of the participants and the scenario of this gunfight, which had no significance whatsoever in the scheme of Western history, are far better known than the names of the participants and the scenario of the Boston Tea Party.

Among the Old West's most hallowed outlaws are Jesse James and Billy the Kid. Neither of them used a boomtown for their operations. They sometimes worked with others, but were individualistic in their styles. They became legends while still living, but neither lived very long. Billy died at twenty-one, Jesse at thirty-two. Jesse had a name that was his, and most of the time a home, but Billy seldom had a home and was known by at least three names—Henry McCarty, William H. Bonney, and William Antrim. Instead of being Robin Hoods, taking from the rich to give to the poor, more often than not they were dead broke, cadging loans from friends and associates.

Today the names of Billy the Kid and Jesse James are known around the world. Their stories, told through the years with the imaginations of hundreds of weavers of tales, bear little resemblance to facts. These two young men, once footnotes in the history of the Old West, now rest somewhere as giants in the mist of America's mythical Valhalla of outlaws and lawmen.

The outlaws and lawmen of the Old West who are well known through popular culture were largely the creation of ink slingers, correspondents, and freelance writers for Eastern newspapers and periodicals. For every Wyatt Earp, Billy the Kid, Jesse James, or Wild Bill Hickok there were dozens of other daring gunmen in big and little towns across the West. If one or the other performed a heroic deed or committed bloody slaughter with no journalist on hand to spread the story across the nation, to create a legend, the event was soon lost in memory or buried in the yellowing pages of an obscure frontier newspaper.

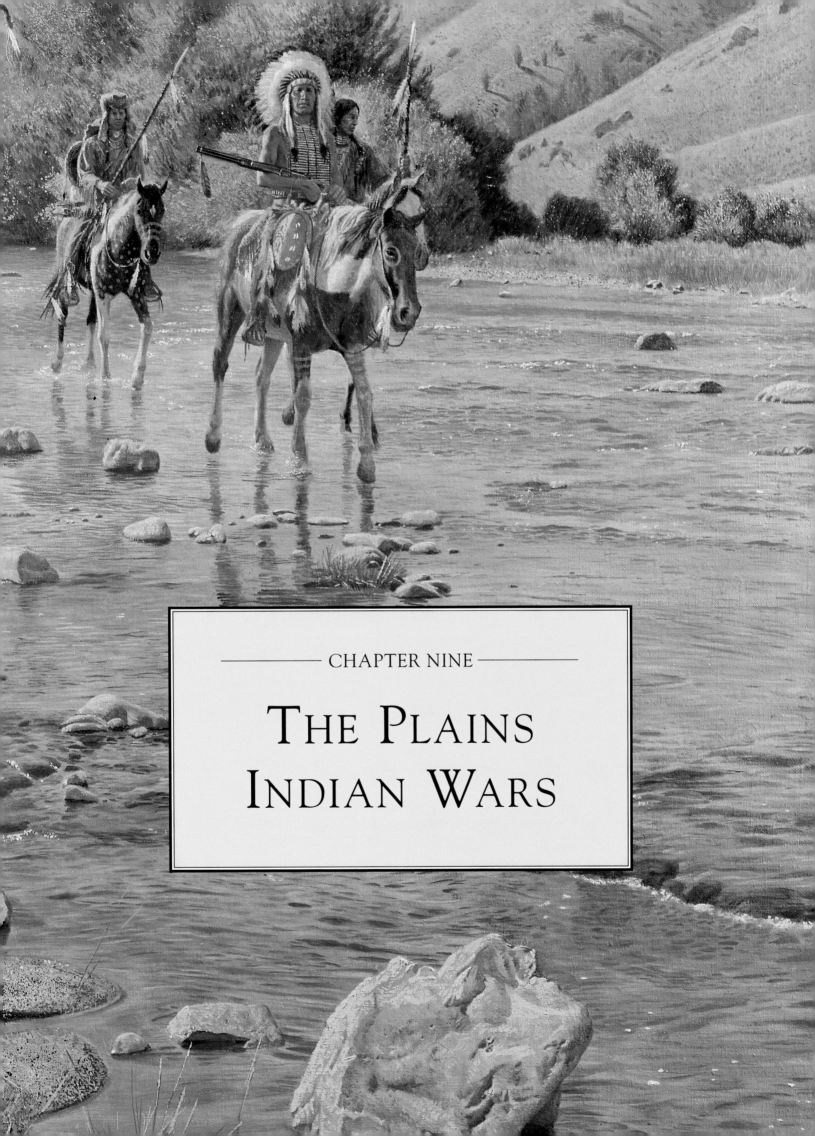

CHAPTER NINE

THE PLAINS
INDIAN WARS

Except for minor conflicts resulting from the economic rivalry of fur traders, relations between Plains Indians and whites were friendly until the occurrence of a single violent action at Fort Laramie in 1854. On August 17, several thousand Brulé and Oglala Sioux were camped around the fort, awaiting the arrival of an Indian agent to distribute the annual supply of goods promised them by the Treaty of 1851. Sometime during that day a caravan of Mormons bound for Salt Lake City passed near a Brulé encampment next to the Oregon Trail. A crippled cow strayed from the wagon train into the camp. A visiting Minneconjou warrior shot the cow and butchered it. The owner of the cow reported the incident to the Fort Laramie commander and demanded restitution.

When the Brulé chief, Conquering Bear, offered horses as payment for the cow, arguments between the commander and the Indians continued for another day. Urged on by a young lieutenant, John Grattan, the commander agreed on the nineteenth to send an armed force to the Brulé camp to arrest the Minneconjou.

Fresh out of West Point, Grattan was eager to make a name for himself. He took twenty-nine of the fort's total of seventy-five soldiers, a drunken interpreter, and two howitzers, and set off down the road to the Brulé camp. Almost five thousand Sioux, twelve hundred of them warriors, were camped in the area. When Grattan reached the Brulé camp, he formed his men and artillery pieces in a line facing the tepee village and asked the chief to surrender the Minneconjou visitor. This the chief refused to do. The Minneconjou stood in front of his friend's tepee, daring the soldiers to fire upon him.

As in so many incidents, no one can say who fired the first shot. But when the soldiers fired their guns in unison and the field pieces blasted metal across the tops of the tepees, panic, fear, and hot anger resulted instantly. Outnumbered by twenty to one, Grattan and his soldiers fled toward the fort, but masses of Oglalas fell upon them in the rear and the Brulés surged after them. Grattan and every man in his command died on the dusty trail, and only the intervention of veteran tribal chiefs stopped the angry Sioux from attacking and destroying the fort.

Participants that day, whose names would become well known through the last half of the nineteenth century, were Red Cloud, Spotted Tail, and Man Afraid of His Horses. They had learned that they could not put their trust in the whites and their blue-coated soldiers. A few years later at Sand Creek their good friends and allies, the Cheyennes, learned the same lesson.

A single outrageous incident sometimes precipitated a lifetime of conflict. Such was the occurrence at Fort Laramie in 1854 that became known as the Grattan Massacre. When an arrogant young lieutenant ordered his men to fire into a Sioux camp after a minor altercation, the Indians retaliated. This ended years of toleration and trust between whites and Indians in the West and initiated a series of Indian wars that did not end until a generation later at Wounded Knee.

The gold that Bill Fairweather found in 1863, creating Montana's Virginia City, brought ten thousand fortune seekers within a few months. The most direct route there, from settled parts of the nation, was the Bozeman Trail from Fort Laramie to Powder River, past the Bighorn Mountains and across the Yellowstone River. This was Sioux and Cheyenne hunting country, and the government had promised it to the Indians "forever" in exchange for their agreement not to interfere with travel and military posts through the route of the Oregon Trail.

The agreement worked well until the Grattan Massacre, but after that many of the young warriors considered white travelers fair game along the Bozeman road. Fortune seekers heading for Montana began traveling in caravans, but even they were constantly harassed. Consequently, in complete disregard of the 1851 treaty, the government decided to offer military protection by building forts along the Bozeman Trail, and ordered the 18th Infantry Regiment to carry out this objective.

The commander of the 18th Infantry was Henry B. Carrington, a forty-two-year-old colonel who had spent the Civil War preparing troops for battle but had never experienced battle himself. He was a methodical man, very religious, a book soldier, and knew nothing about the Indian tribes he was supposed to defend against, and ultimately pacify. In the spring of 1866 the 18th Infantry marched from Nebraska to Fort Laramie, where meetings with leaders from the Plains tribes were to take place.

It soon became apparent that Red Cloud and Man Afraid of His Horses were leading spokesmen for the Sioux, with Red Cloud the dominant figure. When Red Cloud realized that he and his people could not talk Carrington out of violating territory that had been assigned to the tribes, he made a bitter speech during which he pointed an accusing finger at the colonel. Red Cloud's translated words brought some anxiety to the colonel's wife, Margaret. They also brought apprehension to Francis Grummond, wife of a doomed lieutenant. (In her widowhood she would become Carrington's second wife.) Both Margaret and Francis would later record Red Cloud's words in their books about army life. "The Great White Father sends us presents and wants us to sell him the road, but the white chief comes with soldiers to steal it, before the Indians say yes or no. I will talk with you no more. I and my people will go now, and we will fight you."

After Red Cloud and the Sioux angrily departed Fort Laramie, Colonel Carrington led his column of partly mounted infantry north up the Bozeman Trail. Along the way, during this twenty-seven-day march, the troops were occasionally harassed, but after they reached Big Piney Creek, with pine forests and snow-capped Bighorn Mountains off to the west, Carrington knew he had found the site for his main base—Fort Phil Kearny. Between mid-July and the end of October, using wood from the nearby forests, the men of the 18th Infantry built a stockaded fort that an inspecting officer declared to be the best on the frontier. But during those fifteen weeks several lives were lost to the united tribes who were determined to drive these intruders from their treasured hunting lands.

To deal with Indian attacks, Carrington asked for cavalry to add to his mounted infantry. Late in the summer the army assigned two companies of the Second Cavalry Regiment to the fort, but they did not arrive until November. Among the cavalry officers was Lieutenant Horatio Bingham, who a few days after his arrival took his men into an ambush that proved to be fatal to him. Like most of the other officers at Fort Phil Kearny, Bingham knew nothing of Indian guerilla fighting, or their decoy tricks.

Captain William J. Fetterman of the mounted infantry knew no more than Bingham about fighting Indians. He had won honors fighting Confederates with Sherman in Georgia and when he arrived at Fort Phil Kearny he boasted that

Fort Phil Kearny was one of the sturdiest of the stockaded forts in the West—and it may have been the stockade that saved the lives of the surviving defenders after an Indian ambush annihilated Captain William J. Fetterman's command.

The cavalry charge in line, brought to perfection during the Civil War, won the awe and admiration of Indian warriors, some of whom made a study of the bluecoats' tactics—for later use.

with a company of eighty men he could ride through the entire Sioux nation. Neither Carrington nor Fetterman was aware that during the six months since construction began on the fort, Red Cloud had been forming alliances with Cheyennes and Arapahos, as well as with sub-tribes of the Sioux. All through the summer young warriors like Crazy Horse and Sitting Bull had been tantalizing soldiers around the fort and travelers on the Bozeman road. They studied the methods of the soldiers and sharpened their skills at outwitting them.

On the morning of December 21, a small war party of Indians attacked a wood train outside the fort. The attack was a stratagem designed to draw soldiers away from the fort and the Lodge Trail Ridge. Behind the ridge a large force of Indians was gathering. When the soldiers went galloping off to rescue the wood train, a small party of decoys that included Sioux, Cheyenne, and Arapaho appeared on the slope of the Lodge Trail Ridge facing the fort. Among these decoys were three young men who would become famous over the next decade—Crazy Horse, Hump, and Little Wolf. Over the ridge behind the decoys, warriors of the united tribes concealed themselves in gulleys and in the underbrush around Peno Creek.

Meanwhile, Colonel Carrington ironically assigned Captain Fetterman eighty men, some mounted, some on foot, to clear the decoys off the slope of Lodge Trail Ridge. The colonel told Fetterman not to advance beyond the ridge top. Crazy Horse and his companions, however, knew that the ambush was now prepared and the time had come to lure the soldiers into the trap. The Indians taunted the approaching soldiers, trying to stay just out of range of their weapons, waving blankets to frighten their horses, drawing them to the top of the ridge.

Lieutenant Grummond's mounted troop reached the crest first, and he ordered his men to begin firing at the fleeing decoys. When Fetterman's men came alongside, the only Indians they could see were the decoys. The captain evidently decided at this point to disregard Carrington's orders and finish off the scattering young braves.

On an August morning in 1867, Red Cloud and several hundred warriors poured out of the foothills near Fort Phil Kearny to attack soldiers and woodcutters. Unknown to the attackers, hidden behind wagon boxes were soldiers armed with new breech-loading rifles. Many warriors died in what is recorded as the Wagon Box Fight.

With each advance in white settlements, the Plains tribes fought back even harder. Warriors on horseback won the admiration of such observers as the artist George Catlin and the cavalryman and general George Custer.

After the Civil War ended, the army sent several regiments into the West to keep the peace. Among them were regiments of black soldiers, including cavalrymen whom the Indians called "buffalo soldiers." One of their notable feats was the rescue in 1868 of Major Forsyth's men at Beecher Island.

Minutes later, Fetterman and his eighty soldiers were trapped in a swarm of encircling warriors well armed with muskets and bows. Not one soldier survived. The incident was called the Fetterman Massacre, and had George Custer not gone to the Little Big Horn ten years later, overshadowing Fetterman, the event would have much greater significance in the annals of the Indian wars.

During the months following the fight, Red Cloud became the outstanding Plains Indian leader, often compared in the newspapers to Napoleon Bonaparte. Lieutenant-Colonel Henry Wessels replaced Colonel Carrington, who would spend the remainder of his life attempting to justify his actions as commander of Fort Phil Kearny.

But to the Indians the fort was still a hated thing, still standing in the heart of the country that the tribes believed to be theirs. Red Cloud and his followers never relaxed pressure on the garrison, nor on the supply trains and travelers using the Bozeman Trail. With their darting raids they made conditions so dangerous for the fort's woodcutters that full companies had to be sent out to guard the men at work. For defense, they placed several wagon boxes in an oval corral beside the pine woods.

On an August morning several hundred Indians poured suddenly out of the foothills. Woodchoppers and soldiers dashed for the wagon-box corral. Unknown to the Indians, the soldiers were armed with recently issued breech-loading rifles. When the mounted attackers rushed closer, expecting to overrun the wagon boxes as the soldiers paused to reload and use their ramrods, they met continuous rifle fire instead. Many ponies and warriors were shot down. The attackers withdrew, tried one more assault on foot, but could not overcome the fire of the breech-loaders. Years later Red Cloud said that he lost the flower of his young warriors in the Wagon Box Fight.

Nevertheless, guerilla fighting continued around the fort and on the Bozeman road. By springtime of 1868, representatives of the government had decided that guarding an overland route to Montana was not worth the costs. They summoned Red Cloud and other tribal leaders to Fort Laramie. Red Cloud's response was to send a messenger to inform the officials that he would never sign a peace treaty until Fort Phil Kearny was closed and all soldiers were removed from his country. Less than a month later the army issued orders to close the fort and the Bozeman Trail, all soldiers to be transferred to other commands.

When the 18th Infantry marched into northern Wyoming to build Fort Phil Kearny, the Sioux and the Cheyennes considered it a treaty violation and began harassing supply wagons.

At last, after two years of unyielding resistance, Red Cloud had won his war. Through the following stormy decade, the Powder River country would belong to the Plains Indians.

During the rise of Red Cloud, several hundred miles to the southeast a man whose name was to epitomize the sobriquet "Indian fighter" was building his reputation on the plains of Kansas and Nebraska. Known as the "Boy General" during the Civil War (he became a brevet major general at the age of twenty-four) his picture was on the covers of the illustrated weeklies, and sheet music bore his name in the titles of songs.

Like many other officers, Custer had difficulty finding a military assignment in an era of peace. He was galled by constant reminders that the public had forgotten him. Eventually, with the help of his patron, General Phil Sheridan, he was given the permanent rank of lieutenant-colonel and assigned to a new cavalry regiment—the Seventh—organized to fight Indians on the Plains.

During 1867 he campaigned under General Winfield Hancock out of Fort Riley, Kansas. At the close of the campaign, which accomplished little, he came close to wrecking his military career. Instead of remaining with his troops at Fort Wallace, as ordered, he made a hasty journey to Fort Riley to see his wife, Elizabeth. In the court-martial that followed he was charged not only with being absent without leave, but of mistreating his men, executing deserters without trials, overworking regimental horses, and using government equipment for private business. The military court found him guilty on all counts, but instead of being cashiered he was suspended from rank, command, and pay for one year.

His good friend General Sheridan again came to the rescue of the Boy General. Before the end of the year's suspension, Sheridan summoned him back to Kansas to command the Seventh Cavalry in a campaign against Plains tribes camped in Indian Territory. Ironically, the first village the soldiers attacked was that of Black Kettle, who with his wife had miraculously survived Sand Creek four years earlier.

In the fog of a November dawn, Custer and his troopers, with the regimental band blaring martial music, galloped into the peaceful village. Awakened by cries of "Soldiers, soldiers!" Black Kettle mounted his pony, lifted his wife up behind him, and started across a ford on the Washita. At the river's edge, bullets caught him from behind and knocked his wife to the ground beside him. The cavalrymen splashed across the ford, firing at fleeing Cheyennes.

At the end of the action, one hundred and three Cheyennes were dead, only eleven of them warriors. Fifty-three women and children were captured and herded back to the regimental base at Camp Supply, where General Sheridan was awaiting news of the "victory." The returning cavalrymen brought him the scalp of Black Kettle. In his report the general described the dead Cheyenne leader as "a worn-out and worthless old cypher."

Five years after the destruction of Black Kettle's village, Custer and the Seventh Cavalry were stationed at Fort Abraham Lincoln in Dakota Territory. Custer was constantly complaining because he was still a lieutenant-colonel instead of a full colonel, and he was always on the lookout for some means to enhance his reputation. When General Sheridan visited the fort in the spring of 1874, Custer told him about rumors of immense gold deposits in the Black Hills. Because of the Treaty of 1868, non-Indians were forbidden to pass over or reside upon Black

More devastating to the Plains tribes than warfare was the increasing slaughter of buffalo, their basic source of food, shelter, and clothing. During the 1870s a demand for buffalo hides around the world brought hundreds of professional hunters into the Plains. By the end of the decade they had killed entire herds, almost exterminating the species, and destroying the economy and the culture of the Plains tribes.

Hills land, but Custer had learned of a loophole that permitted representatives of the government to enter the Hills "in discharge of duties." To Custer, exploring the Black Hills was a duty to be discharged. If he found gold, the discovery would bring him fame and perhaps the long desired promotion.

In the summer of 1874, with Sheridan's backing, he took an expedition into the Indians' sacred Black Hills. Geologists who accompanied the expedition found both gold and silver. Custer's name was immediately back in newspaper headlines, and within weeks thousands of gold-crazy prospectors were violating the sanctity of the Black Hills and the Treaty of 1868. This created intense Indian hostility, and in an effort to stave off an Indian war, the government offered to buy the Black Hills. To such tribal leaders as Red Cloud, Sitting Bull, and Crazy Horse, this was an insult to their sacred beliefs. The Black Hills were not for sale.

Government officials in Washington now decided the best way to control the Plains tribes was to confine them to reservations. Consequently, the Interior Department, the Indian Bureau, and the War Department began coordinating moves that would make this a permanent Indian policy. On November 5, 1875, a special inspector for the Indian Bureau announced that Plains tribes living outside reservations were well fed and armed, were lofty and independent in their attitudes, and were therefore a threat to the reservation system. He recommended that troops be sent against them during the winter "to whip them into subjection."

Two weeks later the Secretary of War warned of trouble in the Black Hills unless the government ignored the treaty and took possession to protect the white gold miners there. On December 3, the Commissioner of Indian Affairs notified agents assigned to the Plains tribes to order all Indians who were off reservations to report to their assigned agencies by January 31, 1876, or "military force would be sent to compel them."

During the winter of 1875–76, the Indian Bureau and the army, acting as arms of the government, ordered all Plains tribes to go into assigned reservations. Under the leadership of Sitting Bull, Crazy Horse, and others, thousands of Sioux, Cheyennes, and Arapahos gathered along the Little Bighorn, determined to remain free of government control. It was here that Custer found them on June 25, 1876, and fought a battle now known around the world.

On February 1, the Secretary of the Interior notified the Secretary of War that the time had expired for Indians to come into reservations, and that the military were free to take action. A week later, the War Department authorized General Sheridan to begin operations against the Sioux, specifically those who were with Sitting Bull and Crazy Horse. On the following day Sheridan ordered Generals Crook and Terry (Custer's commander) to begin preparations for military operations in the area "where Crazy Horse and his allies frequented."

In February the camps of almost all Plains tribes off reservations were surrounded by deep snow for many miles, making it impossible to travel to any reservation—if the Indians had wished to do so. By early spring the army had organized a three-pronged campaign against the northern Plains tribes, with one column moving from the west, a second from the south, and a third marching westward from Fort Abraham Lincoln. Although General Alfred Terry was commander of that column, he permitted Lieutenant-Colonel Custer to command the Seventh Cavalry, subject to his orders.

When the Seventh Regiment was preparing to leave its assembly point on the Yellowstone River, General Terry gave Custer no definite instructions in regard to his movements, but implied that he was to join forces with General John Gibbons's infantry marching from the west so that the tribes would be unable to escape.

During the morning of June 25, Custer's scouts reported smoke from cooking fires and other signs of Indian encampments in the valley of the Little Bighorn. Late in the morning Custer made his first reckless decision of the day: to disregard Terry's suggestions and attack without waiting for support infantry from the west. Shortly after noon he ordered Captain Frederick Benteen to take one battalion to the left and scout a line of bluffs, a decision that violated a classic principle of war—mass forces. Two hours later, after marching several miles, he sighted dust clouds across the Little Bighorn and feared the Indians were fleeing from his approach. His scouts now warned him that he was facing superior numbers. Custer ignored the warning and violated the principle of security by detaching Major Marcus Reno's battalion, sending it across the Little Bighorn while he continued northwestward with the last battalion. During the next two hours he committed his third violation of the principles of war by allowing himself to be trapped and outnumbered by the warriors of Sitting Bull, Gall, and Crazy Horse.

After leaving Major Reno, Custer continued along high ground on the east side of the river. In the resulting battle he and about two hundred and fifty of his men were overwhelmed by the Sioux and the Cheyennes. Crazy Horse and Gall executed a classic double envelopment, a pincers movement that entrapped Custer's battalion, annihilating the entire force.

Although it was a great victory, the tribal leaders knew that retribution would come. The next time they would be outnumbered. They did not linger on the Little Bighorn, nor try to drive Reno and Benteen off the high ground where they had dug in. Instead they started up the valley toward the Bighorn Mountains, the tribes separating along the way and taking different directions. Crazy Horse and his followers went north of the Black Hills looking for a safe place for a winter camp. Sitting Bull followed the Yellowstone to buffalo country, but eventually led his people to Canada. Many Cheyennes went with Dull Knife to the Powder River country.

During the remainder of the year these holdouts from reservation life were constantly harassed and forced to keep running. They also learned that two of their old heroes, Red Cloud and Spotted Tail, had given up and gone to reservations in Nebraska that were named for them.

The Plains tribes had won their greatest victory in the West, but it brought the wrath of the army and the nation down upon them. Battalions of pursuing troops scattered the fleeing tribespeople who in vain sought refuge. Within a year after the victory over Custer, most of those who had been at the Little Bighorn were forced to become reservation Indians.

CHAPTER TEN

SUNSET FOR THE OLD WEST

To escape being forced upon a reservation, in 1877 the Nez Percé tribe in Oregon attempted flight to Canada. Outnumbered nine to one by soldiers, they were finally trapped in the Bear Paw Mountains after a pursuit of thirteen hundred miles. On October 5, Chief Joseph surrendered to General Nelson Miles and delivered his oft-quoted speech: "From where the sun now stands I will fight no more forever."

After the victory of the tribes at the Little Bighorn, Crazy Horse and his followers traveled north of the Black Hills, but it seemed that every time their hunting parties went in search of buffalo they would narrowly escape confrontation with prowling soldiers. When winter came they made camp on Box Elder Creek. In the camp were many Cheyenne families with warriors who had been part of Crazy Horse's enveloping force around Custer's soldiers.

So it was but natural that after General Ranald McKenzie attacked and destroyed Dull Knife's Cheyenne village on Powder River one freezing November day that the survivors would flee to Crazy Horse's camp. Crazy Horse's people, however, had little food or ammunition to share, and during that winter the combined camp had to move constantly to avoid fights with well-armed soldiers. In January, when General Nelson Miles caught them in the Wolf Mountains, only a miracle enabled most of them to escape into the Bighorns.

By springtime the Sioux and Cheyennes were near starvation. When emissaries came from Red Cloud and Spotted Tail with a promise from General George Crook that Crazy Horse would be given a reservation in Powder River country, he took his nine hundred ragged followers down to Fort Robinson on Red Cloud's reservation and surrendered. All their weapons and ponies were taken from them.

During the summer they lived in canvas tepees and ate the white man's beef and beans. There was talk of a Crazy Horse reservation on the Powder River, but only talk. Rumors spread that young warriors on the Red Cloud and Spotted Tail agencies were planning to join Crazy Horse and flee to the north. Late in the summer the War Department decided to arrest Crazy Horse and ship him to the Dry Tortugas prison off Florida.

On September 6, 1877, Crazy Horse was arrested and brought into Fort Robinson. When he saw that he was to be placed in a barred prison cell he resisted and was stabbed to death. He was the last of the reservation holdouts.

Meanwhile, from the west of the Rocky Mountains, in Idaho, about six hundred and fifty Nez Percé (two hundred and thirty of whom were warriors) were attempting to escape reservation confinement by fleeing to Canada. Because Chief Joseph was well known as a spokesman for the Nez Percé, U.S. government officials viewed him as leader of the flight. Actually, it was his brother Olikut who was the military strategist who led the tribe eastward through Lolo Pass across the Bitterroot Mountains, then south along the Bitterroot River to near disaster at the Big Hole. There, on August 9, General John Gibbon's infantry regiment surprised the Nez Percé before dawn, killing eighty-nine, mostly women and children. After counterattacking, the Nez Percé forced the soldiers on the defensive, although they managed to disengage and move farther south to Camas Meadows. There they found an opportunity to replace some of the pack animals they had lost at the Big Hole. The captured animals were mostly mules belonging to General Oliver O. Howard's soldiers.

Once again the Nez Percé eluded their pursuers and turned east toward Yellowstone, which five years earlier had been established as the first national park. Ironically, General Sherman, the commander of all the U.S. Armies, was vacationing there. When the columns of Nez Percé passed through the park, they were racing toward Canada, and there was little that Sherman could do to halt their progress.

At the start of their flight, the Nez Percé warriors were outnumbered nine to one. Their weapons were inferior in firepower to those of the soldiers. And they were burdened with more than four hundred women and children who had to be protected.

As they left Yellowstone Park, unknown to them two fresh columns of soldiers were moving from the east with orders to halt the Nez Percé before they could reach Canada and freedom. On September 16, troops from the 2nd and 7th Cavalry regiments cut across the pathway of the fleeing tribe, killing twenty-one Nez Percé and capturing many of their ponies. The loss of warriors and the increase in the number of soldiers changed the odds against the Nez Percé to sixteen to one. And they were running out of ammunition for their old trade guns.

Yet the column struggled on toward Canada. In the Bear Paw Mountains, little more than a day's march lay between them and the border, but exhaustion brought them to a halt. General Nelson Miles's troops found them there. The cavalrymen formed a line front and charged the camp. Many casualties were suffered by both sides. After the cavalry retreated, no more Nez Percé war leaders were left alive. Less than a hundred warriors survived. As the ranking leader, Chief Joseph approached General Miles's headquarters under a white flag and asked for peace. During the four days of negotiations, the soldiers brought up artillery and shelled the still defiant Nez Percé encampment.

On October 5, they had traveled thirteen hundred miles on their failed flight to freedom. General Nelson Miles promised the Nez Percé that if they surrendered, they would be returned to a reservation in their homeland. Then Chief Joseph delivered his oft-quoted surrender speech—"From where the sun now stands I will fight no more forever"—which has become an enduring part of American Indian literature.

Through all the traditional hunting grounds of the northern Plains, soldiers continued to track down any Indians off a reservation.

But that was not the end of the Nez Percé's misery. After being herded across Montana to Fort Keogh and then taken by flatboats to Fort Abraham Lincoln, instead of being returned to their homeland, as promised, they were shipped to Indian Territory as exiles. During the seven years that followed, many died of malaria and malnutrition. When at last Chief Joseph persuaded the government to relent and let them go home, only two hundred and eighty-seven of the tribe of six hundred and fifty that had left Idaho were alive to return.

In the spring of 1877, an ordeal similar to that of the Nez Percé began for the Northern Cheyennes. After joining Crazy Horse following the destruction of Dull Knife's village, the Cheyennes endured the winter with the Sioux. When Crazy Horse surrendered at Fort Robinson, Dull Knife, Little Wolf, and other Cheyenne leaders surrendered too. Altogether the Cheyennes numbered about one thousand, and they expected to be given a reservation in the Tongue River country near the one promised to Crazy Horse and his people. No reservation was provided for either tribe, however, and the Indian Bureau decided that the Northern Cheyennes should be sent to Indian Territory to live with their southern tribal relatives. Guarded by soldiers, they traveled overland on foot and horseback for more than three months until they reached Fort Reno on the Southern Cheyenne reservation in Indian Territory.

Their southern relatives were kind to them, but they too had little food, and no medicine to combat malaria and the other diseases that began striking the northerners who, like the Nez Percé, were unaccustomed to the climate. Some of the younger people began talking of returning home. It would be better to die fighting the soldiers who pursued them, they said, than to die of disease and starvation.

On the night of September 9, Dull Knife and Little Wolf, with warriors and their families totaling about three hundred, left their tepees standing and slipped away to the north. The journey that followed was as heroic as the flight of the Nez Percé.

For three days they traveled as though driven by a common will, straining all their physical energies, showing little mercy to their few horses. On the fourth day they crossed the Cimarron, one hundred and fifty miles from their starting point, and stopped to rest in a defensive position of cedar brakes and canyons.

Pursuing soldiers found them there. The captain in command offered the Cheyennes the choice of a fight or returning to the reservation. As spokesman for the tribe, Little Wolf replied that the Cheyennes were going north and would attack no one unless they were attacked first. The foolish captain took his company into the canyon and was immediately pinned down. During the night the Cheyennes slipped away in small parties.

Soon the tribe was in a running battle across Kansas and Nebraska, with cavalrymen galloping in pursuit from five forts, and infantrymen riding in railroad cars back and forth along three parallel tracks. Ten thousand soldiers and three thousand armed civilian volunteers joined the pursuit. The Cheyennes' clothing was in tatters and they were so short of horses that the warriors took turns riding and running on foot.

After the Northern Cheyennes were forcibly removed to Indian Territory several hundred miles away from their homeland, they defied the might of the army in an epic attempt to return home.

Soon after they reached Nebraska, at a night camp the Cheyennes took a head count. Thirty-four of the three hundred who had started were missing, most from the bullets of their pursuers. Dull Knife looked at the half-starved children and weakening old people; they could travel no farther than Red Cloud's reservation, he said, where they would ask for aid at Fort Robinson, the place from which they had started.

Little Wolf scoffed at this. He wanted nothing more to do with soldiers and forts. He was going to the Tongue River country where he could live like a Cheyenne again. The next morning the column divided, about half going with Little Wolf, the others with Dull Knife. Those who went with Dull Knife were imprisoned in a barracks and told they must return to Indian Territory. When they tried to escape, most were wounded and captured. The thirty-eight who did escape were hunted down and bombarded with mountain artillery until only nine were left alive. Six of them escaped, Dull Knife among them. He and his little party went on to Pine Ridge, where they were taken in by the Sioux.

As for Little Wolf's followers, they spent the winter in holes dug in the earth near a tributary of the Niobrara River. In the spring they went to the Tongue River country and surrendered to the soldiers at Fort Keogh. Little Wolf and most of his warriors became scouts for the army. Since there was little to do, they learned to drink whiskey to alleviate their boredom and despair. Eventually the whiskey killed Little Wolf.

In July 1881, Sitting Bull decided to return to the United States with his Hunkpapa people. During the four years they had lived in Saskatchewan, Sitting Bull had been unable to persuade the government to treat them as Canadian Indians, subject to the rights of the Canadian tribes. Each year the wild game grew scarcer, and each year a few of his people would quietly return to the northern Plains country. After four years, there were only one hundred and eighty-six remaining, and in July they crossed the border and surrendered at Fort Buford. Sitting Bull expected to be sent to the Hunkpapa agency at Standing Rock in Dakota Territory, but instead he was taken down the Missouri River to Fort Randall and jailed as a prisoner of war. Not until two years later did Sitting Bull reach Standing Rock to begin his first experience as a reservation Indian, a plight he had despised all his adult life. In the summer of 1885 when Buffalo Bill offered him a role in his Wild West Show, Sitting Bull eagerly accepted in order to get away from Standing Rock and see something of the white people's civilization. One season was enough, however, and he declined an invitation to travel with the show to Europe.

During this decade of the 1880s, the six tribes of Apaches in the Southwest were making their last stands. After the death of Cochise, the Chiricahuas, with their fierce determination to remain free, continued to draw the attention of the nation. The names that sprang from reports and headlines included Victorio, Nana, and Geronimo.

For a decade, into the 1880s, the Chiricahuas and other Apaches held out longer than other Southwestern tribes in their resistance to reservation control.

Because of his insouciance and the easy translations of his earthy Apache sayings that appeared in print, Geronimo was soon known to most Americans. An early follower of Cochise, he was feared and hated in the Southwest, yet was sometimes admired for his tenacity against the greatest odds. In April 1877, he received considerable notice when he and his band of followers were arrested by trickery at Ojo Caliente and taken to the White Mountain reservation at San Carlos. For months he tried to transform himself into a reservation Apache, but other warriors would occasionally leave San Carlos, and often their raids for horses and cattle would be blamed on Geronimo because the press had made his name so well known.

In 1881, Geronimo decided he had endured enough of reservation life. Six months later he and several other Chiricahua leaders returned to San Carlos to free their people. In the flight that followed, six companies of cavalry pursued. In a brilliant rear-guard action the Apaches escaped into Mexico, where disaster struck them. A Mexican infantry regiment attacked them, killing most of the women and children.

After that, Geronimo surrendered to General George Crook, but then left the reservation once again. In 1886, in his last contest with the U.S. Army, Geronimo and twenty-four warriors for four months outwitted General Nelson Miles and his five thousand soldiers, hundreds of civilian militia, five hundred Apache scouts, and hundreds of Mexican soldiers. When the Apache scouts found him, he surrendered his rifle for the last time. He and his people were shipped to Florida and Alabama, where many died of tuberculosis and malaria. In 1894, the few survivors were given a home with the Kiowas and Comanches in Indian Territory.

Throughout the West during the 1880s, as tribe after tribe was locked up on reservations, waves of despair swept over a people that no longer could control their own lives. The chiefs had been shorn of their power. The buffalo had vanished. The ceremonies of life and renewal had lost their meaning.

Geronimo fled reservation life three times, but finally, in 1886, he surrendered for the last time.

In times of despair new religions are born. Prophets true and false arose among the Apaches, the Nez Percé, the Crows, and Kiowas. In Nevada a Paiute named Wovoka devised a new religion of the dance. In a matter of months the Ghost Dance spread across the West, especially among the Plains tribes. In the spring of 1890, the Sioux began dancing the Ghost Dance at Pine Ridge, Red Cloud's reservation.

Followers of the Ghost Dance religion believed that if they danced and sang ghost songs, one day they would be raised into the air while a new earth would bury all the white people. After that, great herds of buffalo and horses would appear, and then they would be set down among their ancestors on a new land where only Indians would live.

Although Sitting Bull was dubious about the dead returning to life, he thought the new religion might be good for his despairing people, and he did not oppose teachers of the dance when they came to Standing Rock. James McLaughlin, the Indian agent, viewed the religion as "pernicious." At Pine Ridge, Indian agent Daniel Royer was so frightened by the night-long dances that he sought protection from the army, an action that precipitated the disaster that followed.

At Standing Rock, McLaughlin sent agency policemen to arrest Sitting Bull, and during a scuffle this stubborn icon of the Plains tribes was killed. The effect upon all tribes in the area was terror, panic, and flight. Big Foot (Spotted Elk) and three hundred and fifty Minneconjou and other Sioux, two hundred and thirty of them women and children, fled toward Pine Ridge. On December 29, 1890, at Wounded Knee Creek, when soldiers of the 7th Cavalry attempted to disarm them; a gun was fired, probably accidentally, and deadly fire from the soldiers resulted in a massacre. One hundred and forty-six Sioux were killed, and many wounded. Twenty-five soldiers died from their own comrades' fire and in hand-to-hand fighting.

Wounded Knee marked the end of the long and bloody Indian wars, and the beginning of the end of the Old West.

Early in the nineteenth century, pressures from white settlers in the southeastern United States led to the creation of Indian Territory—what is now the state of Oklahoma. Cherokees, Creeks, Choctaws, Chickasaws, and Seminoles traveled to the territory over their various "trails of tears" and were assigned land with the native Osages, Comanches, and Kiowas. During the years that followed, many other tribes in the West were forced to move there to occupy land that they were told would be Indian Territory forever.

Adjusting to reservation life was a slow process, more difficult for the old than for the young.

On April 22, 1889, an event occurred that signaled the end of the Old West—the opening of land to settlement in what had been Indian Territory. At high noon, thousands of land seekers gathered along the border and at the firing of a signal gun they began a mad dash to drive claim stakes into ground once assigned "forever" to Indian tribes.

Laws supposedly protected the Indians from white incursions, but the government provided rights-of-way for railroads and permitted the army to build several forts. Texans, who had driven their cattle herds north over authorized trails, were soon demanding the right to graze their cattle on tribal grasslands. And the men who built the railroads across fertile unoccupied lands began returning as illegal homesteaders. "Boomers," they were called, and tribal leaders protested and demanded their removal.

Acceding to the cries from would-be homesteaders for more land, in 1889 President Benjamin Harrison authorized the opening of unoccupied land in Indian Territory and the purchase of land from the tribes. In the early spring of that year more than fifty thousand participants gathered for the first of several "runs" to claim farmland and city lots on two million acres that had once been "Indian Territory forever." Now it would be known as Oklahoma.

On April 22, as high noon approached, the thousands of land seekers assembled along the Kansas-Oklahoma border—on foot, on horseback, in buggies and covered wagons. Soldiers guarded the line to see that no one gained advantage over another. Signal guns were fired, and the mobs of claimants rushed across the border—running, galloping, shouting, rolling forward to drive claim stakes. Before sundown the swarm of immigrants laid claim to thousands of homesteads and town lots.

Following this occupation of Indian lands, the Bureau of Census report for 1890 declared that the unsettled area of the United States "has been so broken into by isolated bodies of settlement that there can hardly be said to be a frontier line." Differences between settled and unsettled land, therefore, could no longer have a place in the census reports. The frontier was closed.

At a meeting of historians in July 1893, in Chicago, a thirty-two-year-old professor spoke on the significance of the frontier in American history. His name was Frederick Jackson Turner, and among the things he said was that the frontier experience and the abundance of free land had created a society that was energetic and self-reliant.

Certainly in the decade of the 1890s Americans reluctantly watched the Old West disappear. William Frederick Cody, who as Buffalo Bill had become a national image of the Old West, used his Wild West Show to tap into the country's nostalgia for cowboys and Indians, stagecoaches and covered wagons. Organized in the 1880s, the show's popularity soared into the early twentieth century. Audiences adored the King of the Cowboys, the Cowboy Kid, and Little Sure Shot Annie Oakley. They applauded the U.S. Cavalry's rescue of the Deadwood Stage from an Indian attack. They cheered Pony Express relay races, rodeo performances by the Rough Riders, and re-enactments of Custer's Last Stand. They hissed and booed the real Sitting Bull during his one-year season with the show.

In 1883, a twenty-five-year-old well-to-do native of Manhattan journeyed to Dakota Territory for a buffalo hunt. His name was Theodore Roosevelt and he quickly fell under the spell of ranch life and the Great Plains. A year later both

In the last years of the nineteenth century, settlers swarmed into the farmlands of the West to establish homesteads. In 1890 the Census Bureau declared that there was no longer a frontier line, no longer an Old West.

In 1898, Teddy Roosevelt, who proved himself as a rancher in Dakota Territory, organized a regiment of Rough Riders for service during the Spanish-American War. The newspapers delighted in his charge up a hill in Cuba and made him a hero to the nation. Two years later he was elected Vice President. After President McKinley's assassination, Roosevelt became President of the United States—the first cowboy in the White House.

his wife and his mother died. In an attempt to allay his grief he returned to Dakota and started life anew as a rancher.

Roosevelt believed in the strenuous life and soon overcame the prejudices of even the roughest of the frontier populace by displaying courage, tenacity, and a sense of humor. In 1886, he returned to the East to marry a childhood sweetheart and honeymoon in Europe. During the winter that he was away from his ranch, a series of great blizzards wiped out cattle herds across the Plains. Like many of his neighbors, Roosevelt suffered staggering financial losses.

To recoup his fortune, Roosevelt returned to New York. He was soon involved in politics, and when war with Spain began in 1898, he set about raising a cavalry regiment of cowboys from the West. He borrowed the regiment's name from his friend William F. Cody's Wild West Show—the Rough Riders.

And so, by leading a charge up a hill in Cuba, Teddy Roosevelt rode into the vice-presidency with President William McKinley. When McKinley was assassinated, Teddy the Rough Rider was suddenly President of the nation. For the first time in history, a cowboy occupied the White House. The Old West appeared to be in a state of recuperation.

Meanwhile, the popularity of Buffalo Bill's Wild West Show and the Congress of Rough Riders was beginning a slow decline. In his seasonal openings in Madison Square Garden, Cody began inviting such famous westerners as George Custer's widow, Elizabeth, to appear with him, and he added a new spectacle—Roosevelt's charge up a slope during the Battle of San Juan Hill.

During the early years of the new century, several of Cody's best assistants retired or died, and in 1906 he entered the sixtieth year of his life. His horsemanship and marksmanship began rapidly to decline. The departure of Teddy Roosevelt, the Rough Rider, from the White House in 1909 seemed to coincide with the dying spirit of the Wild West Show. In an effort to keep the show alive, Cody joined with Pawnee Bill's extravaganza of Far Eastern spectacles.

For three years the combined show thrived, but much of the Old West had gone out of it. By 1913 Cody had lost control of his show, and in September his creditors held an auction. The items most in demand were relics of the Old West—prairie schooners, silver-mounted saddles, trained horses, even the handmade drum that Cody had received from Sitting Bull when he left the show.

To keep busy, Cody went into the burgeoning movie business and recovered some of his lost fortune. Buffalo Bill's Wild West was gone forever, however, as was the Old West from which it had come.

Symbolic of the passage of the Old West is this skeleton of a chuck wagon—no longer needed for roundups or trail drives to cowtowns.

THE IMAGES

Two Feathers, 1985 (page 1)
Oil on board, 9 x 11½ inches
Mr. and Mrs. Bennett Weil

Daniel Boone, 1984 (page 8)
Mixed media, 15 x 13½ inches
Hammer Galleries, N.Y.C.

Morning Mist, 1981 (pages 2–3)
Oil on canvas, 30 x 40 inches
Mr. and Mrs. Jack Morse

Chief High Horse, 1985 (page 11)
Oil on canvas, 20 x 16 inches
Mr. and Mrs. Bennett Weil

Near Old Tucson, 1973 (page 5)
Oil on canvas, 28 x 32 inches
San Lee Brassner Gallery, Palm Beach, FL

Lamar Valley, Yellowstone, 1989 (pages 12–13)
Oil on canvas, 18 x 24 inches
Collection of the artist

And Then One Day the Circus Came to Town, 1980 (pages 6–7)
Oil on canvas, 30 x 40 inches
Mr. Leonard Strear

Ancestors of the Paiute, 1976 (pages 14–15)
Oil on canvas, 28 x 40 inches
Favell Museum, Klamath Falls, OR

Haida Bear Dance, 1987 (pages 16–17)
Oil on canvas, 36 x 52 inches
Collection of the artist

Lewis and Clark, 1985 (pages 24–25)
Mixed media, 14½ x 20½ inches
Hammer Galleries, N.Y.C.

Big Head Dancer of the Pomo, 1979 (page 17)
Oil on canvas, 20 x 16 inches
Lowie Museum of Anthropology, Berkeley, CA

Man and His Mountain, 1982 (pages 26–27)
Oil on canvas, 16 x 20 inches
Mr. and Mrs. Elisha Cohen

Los Conquistadores, 1981 (pages 18–19)
Oil on board, 16 x 20 inches
Mr. and Mrs. Robert Anderson

The First Bank Charter of Missouri, 1981 (pages 28–29)
Oil on canvas, 30 x 40 inches
Landmark Bancshares Corp., St. Louis, MO

Apache Roundup, 1979 (pages 20–21)
Oil on canvas, 25 x 33 inches
Mr. C. Henry Roath

Night Watch, 1981 (page 30)
Oil on board, 22¾ x 30 inches
Mr. T. G. Rogers

Discovery of San Francisco Bay, 1987 (pages 22–23)
Oil on canvas, 34 x 50 inches
Collection of the artist

Moving On, 1983 (page 31)
Oil on canvas, 30 x 40 inches
San Lee Brassner Gallery, Palm Beach, FL

Tomahawk Throwing Contest, 1981 (pages 32–33)
Oil on canvas, 36 x 54 inches
Mr. Robert E. Torray

Crossing the River, 1988 (pages 42–43)
Oil on canvas, 26 x 46 inches
John Gammill Co., Oklahoma City, OK

Westward Ho!, 1987 (pages 34–35)
Oil on canvas, 32 x 44 inches
John Gammill Co., Oklahoma City, OK

Storm Clouds, 1978 (page 45)
Oil on canvas, 34 x 25 inches
Glenbow Museum, Calgary, Canada

The Singer Family, 1981 (pages 36–37)
Oil on canvas, 36 x 48 inches
Mr. and Mrs. Craig Singer

Splitting the Herd, 1988 (pages 46–47)
Oil on canvas, 32 x 54 inches
Mr. Pierson M. Grieve

Prairie Kitchen, 1987 (pages 38–39)
Oil on canvas, 30 x 40 inches
John Gammill Co., Oklahoma City, OK

Santa Fe Trail, 1986 (pages 48–49)
Mixed media, 15¾ x 17¼ inches
Hammer Galleries, N.Y.C.

Emily, 1983 (pages 40–41)
Oil on canvas, 28 x 36 inches
Dunnegan Gallery of Art, Bolivar, MO

Fall of the Alamo, 1988 (pages 50–51)
Oil on canvas, 30 x 56 inches
Mr. and Mrs. Craig Singer

Wagons to Yuma, 1983 (pages 52–53)
Oil on canvas, 26 x 34 inches
Mr. and Mrs. Craig Singer

Flying Cloud Clipper Ship, 1985 (pages 62–63)
Mixed media, 15½ x 18 inches
Hammer Galleries, N.Y.C.

When Dust Means Trouble, 1974 (pages 54–55)
Oil on board, 24¾ x 32 inches
Robin Farkis

Tappan's Burro, 1982 (pages 64–65)
Oil on canvas, 22 x 30 inches
Dr. Glenn Gade

First Christmas, 1988 (pages 56–57)
Oil on canvas, 26 x 34 inches
John Gammill Co., Oklahoma City, OK

The Pony Express, 1985 (page 66)
Opaque watercolor, 8¼ x 9½ inches
Saks Galleries, Denver, CO

Running Late, 1978 (pages 58–59)
Oil on canvas, 24 x 30 inches
Glenbow Museum, Calgary, Canada

Mule Train, 1980 (pages 68–69)
Oil on canvas, 22 x 28 inches
Mr. and Mrs. Vincent Bellitte

Gold Discovered at Sutter's Mill, 1995 (page 60)
Opaque watercolor, 14¼ x 12⅞ inches
Hammer Galleries, N.Y.C.

Stage Coach Holdup, 1974 (pages 70–71)
Oil on canvas, 28 x 38 inches
Favell Museum, Klamath Falls, OR

Coming Through the Pass, 1980 (pages 72–73)
Oil on canvas, 28 x 35 inches
Applebranch, Winchester, VA

The Challenge, 1979 (pages 82–83)
Oil on canvas, 25 x 32½ inches
Hammer Galleries, N.Y.C.

In the Shadows, 1982 (pages 74–75)
Oil on canvas, 24½ x 32 inches
Mr. and Mrs. Bernard Haber

Cheyenne Winter, 1981 (pages 84–85)
Oil on canvas, 28 x 38 inches
Mr. Robert E. Torray

First to the Guns, 1992 (pages 76–77)
Oil on canvas, 18 x 30 inches
Dunnegan Gallery of Art, Bolivar, MO

Treaty Talk, 1979 (pages 86–87)
Oil on canvas, 25 x 32 inches
Glenbow Museum, Calgary, Canada

Apache Scout, 1978 (page 78)
Oil on canvas, 20 x 16 inches
Mr. and Mrs. Howard Weingrow

The Movement West, 1859, 1975 (pages 88–89)
Oil on board, 20¼ x 26 inches
Exxon Corporation

Apache Feet Leave No Tracks, 1983 (pages 80–81)
Oil on canvas, 25 x 32 inches
Mr. Douglas R. Phillips

Outlaw Brand, 1971 (page 90)
Oil on board, 20 x 16 inches
Private collection

The Race, 1984 (pages 92–93)
Oil on canvas, 25 x 36 inches
Mr. Victor Niederhoffer

Riding Point, 1982 (page 102)
Oil on canvas, 20 x 16 inches
Mr. Steven Adams

Gen. William Tecumseh Sherman, 1991 (page 94)
Oil on board, 10 x 11½ inches
Collection of the artist

After the Rain, 1981 (pages 104–105)
Oil on board, 22¾ x 30 inches
Mr. Howard M. Bender

Hold Up of Old No. 8, 1987 (pages 96–97)
Oil on canvas, 28 x 38 inches
Hammer Galleries, N.Y.C.

Dry Gulch Canyon, 1973 (pages 106–107)
Oil on canvas, 28 x 38 inches
Dr. Donald Koppel

The Golden Spike, 1985 (pages 98–99)
Mixed media, 8 x 9 inches
Hammer Galleries, N.Y.C.

Blizzard Range, 1972 (page 108)
Oil on board, 22 x 17
Private collection

Wild Horse Mesa, 1982 (pages 100–101)
Oil on canvas, 26 x 34 inches
Mrs. Frank Dickstein

Home, Home on the Range, 1983 (page 109)
Oil on canvas, 28 x 36 inches
Mr. and Mrs. Vincent Bellitte

Lightning Stampede, 1981 (pages 110–111)
Oil on board, 16 x 20 inches
Mr. Steven Wallace

Losing the Trail, 1985 (pages 120–121)
Oil on canvas, 20 x 26 inches
Mr. William Coll

Stir Up the Dust, 1972 (pages 112–113)
Oil on board, 24 x 43 inches
Private collection

The Homestead Act, 1862, 1985 (pages 122–123)
Mixed media, 16 x 18½ inches
Hammer Galleries, N.Y.C.

Early Crossing, 1978 (pages 114–115)
Oil on canvas, 24 x 36 inches
Glenbow Museum, Calgary, Canada

The Kansan, 1973 (page 124)
Oil on board, 33 x 26 inches
Dr. and Mrs. Sigfried Rosenbaum

Early Snow, 1973 (pages 116–117)
Oil on board, 28½ x 38 inches
Palestine High School, Palestine, TX

Fighting Kid from Eldorado, 1971 (page 125)
Oil on board, 21 x 16 inches
Private collection

Boundary Line, 1980 (page 119)
Oil on board, 33 x 25 inches
Mrs. Harry Glass

Sunrise, 1982 (pages 126–127)
Oil on canvas, 24 x 32 inches
Mr. Stacy B. Lloyd, III

The Free Lands, 1972 (page 128)
Oil on board, 20 x 16 inches
Palestine High School, Palestine, TX

The Trail That Leaves None, 1983 (pages 138–139)
Oil on canvas, 28 x 36 inches
Mr. and Mrs. Lou Frederick

Law Killer, 1973 (pages 130–131)
Oil on board, 22 x 29 inches
Private collection

Brave Warrior, 1979 (page 140)
Oil on board, 21 x 17 inches
Mr. and Mrs. Roy Lawrence

Bringing in the Prisoner, 1980 (pages 132–133)
Oil on canvas, 24 x 34½ inches
Glenbow Museum, Calgary, Canada

Fort Suicide, 1972 (page 143)
Oil on board, 22 x 16 inches
Private collection

New Girls in Town, 1983 (pages 134–135)
Oil on canvas, 30 x 40 inches
Mr. and Mrs. Craig Singer

Charge!, 1981 (pages 144–145)
Opaque watercolor, 15½ x 27¾ inches
Mrs. Frank Dickstein

Riders of the Whistling Skull, 1972 (page 137)
Oil on board, 21 x 16 inches
Private collection

Surprise Attack, 1973 (pages 146–147)
Oil on canvas, 30 x 40 inches
Glenbow Museum, Calgary, Canada

War Cry, 1979 (pages 148–149)
Oil on canvas, 19 x 34 inches
Whereabouts unknown

Survivors, 1981 (page 157)
Oil on canvas, 20 x 16 inches
Mr. Robert E. Torray

Buffalo Soldiers, 1993 (page 150)
Opaque watercolor, 12 x 8½ inches
United States Postal Service

The Vanishing American, 1981 (pages 158–159)
Oil on board, 22¾ x 30 inches
Huide Shipping, Inc., Fort Lauderdale, FL

Last Man Alive, 1976 (page 151)
Oil on board, 20 x 16 inches
Private collection

Chief Joseph Surrenders, 1985 (page 160)
Mixed media, 15⅞ x 17¼ inches
Hammer Galleries, N.Y.C.

Thundering Herd, 1982 (pages 152–153)
Oil on board, 23 x 30 inches
Mr. and Mrs. Bernard Haber

When You Can't Hide Tracks, 1982 (pages 162–163)
Oil on canvas, 22 x 30 inches
Mr. Robert P. Lockwood, III

Custer's Last Stand, 1986 (pages 154–155)
Oil on canvas, 34 x 56 inches
Mr. Robert E. Mullane

Painted Horse, 1981 (page 164)
Oil on canvas, 20 x 16 inches
Mr. and Mrs. Harold Bernstein

Apache Raiding Party, 1885, 1978 (pages 166–167)
Oil on canvas, 22 x 31 inches
Glenbow Museum, Calgary, Canada

Oklahoma Land Rush, April 22, 1889, 1988 (pages 172–173)
Oil on canvas, 22 x 50 inches
John Gammill Co., Oklahoma City, OK

Bringing in Geronimo, 1984 (pages 168–169)
Oil on canvas, 25 x 34 inches
Mr. Manfred Demenus

Wild Asp Cabin, 1983 (pages 174–175)
Oil on canvas, 22 x 20 inches
The Kiva, Beaver Creek, CO

The Future, The Past, 1985 (page 170)
Oil on canvas, 20 x 16 inches
Hammer Galleries, N.Y.C.

Rough Riders, 1984 (pages 176–177)
Oil on canvas, 24 x 32 inches
National Guard Bureau, The Pentagon

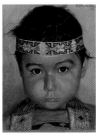

Beaded Headband, 1985 (page 171)
Oil on panel, 10 x 8¼ inches
St. Lifer Art Exchange, Summit, NJ

Still Being Used, 1983 (pages 178–179)
Oil on canvas, 16 x 20 inches
Mr. Charles Gates

INDEX